December 2000

A family tradition...

Love,

Christine

and

Joel

SEASIDE

SEASIDE

Text and photography by
STEVEN BROOKE

PELICAN PUBLISHING COMPANY
Gretna 1999

First printing, March 1995
Second printing, August 1995
Third printing, January 1997
Fourth printing, January 1999

Library of Congress Cataloging-in-Publication Data

Brooke, Steven.
    Seaside / text and photography by Steven Brooke.
        p.   cm.
    ISBN 0-88289-996-1.—ISBN 0-88289-997-X (pbk.)
    1. New towns—Florida—Seaside. 2. Seaside (Fla.)—Buildings,
structures, etc. 3. Seaside Community Development Corporation
(Seaside, Fla.) I. Title.
    NA9053.N4B76 1995
    720'.9759'41—dc20
                                                              94-20911
                                                                  CIP

Photo on p. 1 and p. 3: The Tupelo Street Beach Pavilion,
    designed by Ernesto Buch.
Photo on p. 2: View to the sea from the Pensacola Street Beach
    Pavilion.
Photo on p. 6: Some of Seaside's many towers.

Printed in Hong Kong

Published by Pelican Publishing Company, Inc.
1000 Burmaster Street, Gretna, Louisiana 70053

Porch of the Dreamsicle Cottage looking to the Avarett Tower.

For
Suzanne and Miles

and for my Uncle Paul,
and Robert, Daryl, Micah, and Bud Davis

ACKNOWLEDGMENTS

I wish to thank my friend and colleague Laura Cerwinske, whose advice and editing has been invaluable.

Carmel Modica was Seaside's coordinator of marketing and public relations for seven years. Without her support and patience, the photographic documentation of Seaside would not have proceeded as efficiently.

I would like to acknowledge Seaside's staff, associates, homeowners, and merchants for their hospitality, generosity, and patience with my campaign mentality. I am especially indebted to Christopher A. Kent, Jacqueline Joyce Barker, James Pinckard, Donna Marie Spiers, Betty Rossbach, and Erica Meyers for their assistance with the research and editing; to former Seaside staff members Nancy Patrie and Bonnie Leigh; to former Seaside Institute Director Richard Storm; to Charlotte Thompson, for my lessons in North Florida botany; and to the Modicas for their friendship and unending supply of Cracker Jacks.

My thanks to Dr. Milburn Calhoun, publisher and president of Pelican Publishing Company, my editor, Nina Kooij, and the staff of Pelican for their interest and support. My thanks also to John Rogers for bringing this project to Pelican Publishing Company.

Finally, my deepest thanks to Robert and Daryl Davis. Apart from entrusting me with the documentation of Seaside, their counsel and vision have clarified my artistic direction and strengthened my personal convictions.

INTRODUCTION

I count among my halcyon days the summers spent at Charlotte, the Lake Ontario beach town near Rochester, New York. I still vividly recall morning walks to the beach past the red brick beach pavilion, buying a toy boat at Jack's Corner Market, riding the merry-go-round (with brass ring dispenser!), and, more importantly, the gravity of my concern over which new flavor would be offered that day at Abbott's Custard Stand. (I craved the coffee, detested the sherbets.) Much of that landscape has vanished. Fortunately, the pavilion has been restored and Abbott's Custard Stand continues to inspire and satisfy new generations of four-year-olds. Even after forty-five years, my trips to Rochester always begin at Charlotte.

Author Willie Morris, one of an extraordinary number of inspired writers to come from Mississippi, once wrote about how the unique character of his state promoted the formation of "real" memory. He believed this memory indispensable to producing great literature. Sadly, those "mystic chords of memory" (in Lincoln's words) are not at all cultivated today by the design of our increasingly homogeneous towns and cities.

A numbing sameness pollutes our nation's landscape. We are confronted by an endless parade of faceless shopping malls, taco stands, tire stores, and modular branch banks. Fly to almost any city in the country, rent a car, drive for ten minutes, and—temperature or street names aside—wonder if you have traveled at all.

Equally dismaying is the proliferation of high-rise buildings that are totally out of character and scale with their neighborhoods. At once, the smaller buildings appear vulnerable, then expendable. Rapid changes in tax and zoning laws often follow, promoting even further overpowering development. The charming neighborhoods that originally attracted people, and provided the background and substance of memory for generations, are irreversibly compromised and ultimately reduced to *only* a memory. The sense of human architectural scale—an incisive measure of the quality of life—is lost forever.

The issue is not simplistically one of style: a battle between the "unsympathetic forces" of modernism and the "sanctified champions" of classicism. Clearly, such modernist-era buildings as the three- to eight-story Art Deco hotels along Miami Beach's Ocean Drive do create a splendid urban fabric; and, in their midst, a twenty-story building of any style would be wholly out of place,

VENICE: *Even though the buildings in this Venetian neighborhood differ in style, their harmonious proportions create a pleasurable and humane environment.*

CORAL GABLES: *The beautifully detailed and thoughtfully proportioned historic bank on Coral Way is dwarfed by two prefabricated-concrete high-rise hotels. The scale of the avenue, originally defined by two- to three-story buildings, has been desecrated.*

even if it were otherwise flawlessly designed. The issue is not style but scale.

Coral Gables, Florida, was transformed by just such a process. Begun in the 1920s, it was a thoughtfully planned, Mediterranean Revival-styled city featuring such picturesque materials as handmade barrel roof tiles and locally quarried coral rock. The city building code even included a covenant that precluded sameness of architectural design. However, founder George Merrick's inspired vision was doomed in the early 1970s by the erection of the first glass-walled, high-rise office building. Within a few years, such landmarks as the Coral Gables First National Bank were dwarfed by prefabricated concrete buildings of lumbering proportions, often turned vampire-green at night by mercury floodlights. Also integral to Merrick's city plan were his sublime fountains and

entrances. They enhanced the romantic allure of the Gables by providing elements of procession, grandeur, and human scale to the streets and boulevards. Now, immediately adjacent high-rises and rapidly aging modern apartments mock the largest of these graceful landmarks.

The disfigurement of Coral Gables proceeded even with the existence of an Architectural Review Board. The City Commission approved Board-recommended changes in zoning ordinances that allow even *taller* buildings so long as they are designed "in the Mediterranean Style." The resulting structures have only a cursory relationship to authentic Mediterranean architecture or even to Merrick's version of Mediterranean Revival. The modernist behemoths have merely been replaced by larger, pseudo-Spanish ones.

Coconut Grove, Florida, originally a quiet, unassuming fishing village, was long a favorite of artists, musicians, writers, and designers. Following the destruction of several older, downtown low-rise buildings in the early 1970s, the Grove was quickly inundated with high-rises of fatuous design and appallingly cheap construction. The Grove's main streets now feature trite, postmodern office buildings, condominiums, and an ersatz Mayan hotel. A sprawling, ceaselessly ornate shopping complex turns inward, totally denying the village tradition of on-the-street, storefront shopping. A four-story shopping mall built along Commodore Plaza (a beautiful treelined street of one- and two-story shops) now stands deserted and decaying only four years after its construction because its designers ignored basic principles of urban design, retail planning, and human nature. In less than a generation, much of the downtown area of the Grove was transformed from an intimate village into something utterly common and commercial.

AT RIGHT:
MIAMI BEACH DECO DISTRICT: *The modernist buildings of Ocean Drive are integrated into the urban context because of their pedestrian scale.*

In Spartanburg, South Carolina, the dire, fourteen-story Spartan Foods Tower was built in the center of the historic downtown district. It dwarfs not only the older, three- and four-story buildings but the church as well. In the shadow of the Tower, the historic buildings look like pieces of a train set. If this Tower were placed in the established downtown area of any relatively large city, it would no doubt go unnoticed. In Spartanburg, though, how much more appropriate a grouping of lower-scaled, interconnected buildings would have been. Such an architectural solution would have still revitalized the region, and, by example, would have encouraged patterns of growth that would preserve the scale of the historic downtown district.

SPARTANBURG: *The Spartan Foods Tower ruinously dominates the smaller-scaled buildings of Spartanburg's historic downtown.*

Regrettably, development of this type may become a paradigm for business relocation activity, particularly in our smaller towns. The necessity for infusion of economic activity in any community—particularly in smaller and/or depressed regions—is not at issue. What *is* at issue is the incontestable responsibility of any corporation to analyze the architectural heritage of the town in which it is planning to build, and its obligation to respond sympathetically.

In spite of these transgressions, we may be encouraged by the growing awareness of the dangers of undisciplined, shortsighted development. In the French Quarter of New Orleans, in the historic sections of Charleston and Savannah, in towns like Natchez, Mississippi (where Ron and Mimi Miller and the Historic Natchez Foundation struggle to protect the Natchez Riverfront), and in such major world cities as Rome, Florence, Venice, and Washington, D.C., communities work to maintain the mandated height restrictions that prevent the design of overpowering, infill buildings. In the Art Deco District of Miami Beach, which has suffered the loss of many historic buildings, efforts continue to thwart the development of a large convention-style hotel in the "Bass Museum District," a project that would have devastating effects on the character of this neighborhood. Increasingly, we read reports of communities nationwide that are lobbying against the construction of the large shopping malls that drain the life out of their downtown areas.

As Robert Davis, the developer of Seaside, wrote in his statement to the Mayors' Institute for City Design:

A street in Seaside.

The institutional forces pushing American urbanism further away from the type of town that Seaside represents are large, weighty and have considerable momentum. Nevertheless, there is a strong and widespread revulsion to the symptoms of urban blight. . . .

If this general, unfocused revulsion can be turned into a positive vision of an alternative, there may be some hope for viable and livable American cities and towns. . . . A significant number of people are moving back to the older sections of cities where traditional city life still exists, and they are renovating and reviving these neighborhoods. They are "voting with their feet" and eventually their message will be heard by developers and planning and zoning officials; that these traditional patterns of urbanism are still valid and that we can develop compact, heterogeneous towns and imbue them with a sense of neighborhood and of human scale.

I wish this book to serve as my personal clarion call—an adamant reminder of how our lives are unalterably affected by our architectural surroundings, and of how quickly that fabric can change. It is realistic to hope that Seaside will continue to contribute to this growing awareness. If visitors will take their experiences back to their communities, and if those responsible for the construction of large-scale architectural projects will reassess their goals in light of the accomplishments at Seaside, we may justifiably be optimistic about controlling land development and saving the neighborhoods that enrich our memories and nurture our lives.

BY THE SEA

In 1946, on one of his family's summer pilgrimages, Birmingham department store owner J. S. Smolian bought a remote eighty acres near the tiny hamlet of Seagrove Beach on Florida's northwest Gulf Coast. While a main road led from U.S. 98 down to the beach, only narrow, overgrown, dirt paths led to his land. Smolian's family was incredulous at his foolish investment—$100 per acre for sand and scrub.

J. S. Smolian's progressive intention was to build an employee summer camp that he would call Dreamland Heights. The name accurately reflected his visionary nature. His business partner, however, wanted nothing to do with what seemed a completely worthless piece of land and an equally worthless venture.

The family came to the Gulf Shore every summer. When Panama City Beach became too crowded, they stayed at Seagrove Beach. Occasionally, Smolian would take them to the fields at the western edge of Seagrove Beach, where they would wander around his wild tract of land and talk about his plans for Dreamland Heights.

In 1969, Smolian finally decided to develop the land. He first discussed with representatives of the University of Alabama his ideas for a conference center with neighboring, small cottages. He reasoned that an idyllic beach location and the prestige of University sponsorship would make a well-run conference center very competitive. Unfortunately, economic and political conditions never favored the idea, and Smolian's dream never materialized. A decade later, however, his grandson, Robert Davis, conceived an idea more visionary than even J. S. Smolian dreamed.

AT LEFT:
A tract of undeveloped land along the North Florida Panhandle.

ROBERT DAVIS

Robert Davis grew up in Birmingham, Alabama. He spent his summers on the Gulf Coast and each year joined his family on their yearly trek to his grandfather's property. After studying history at Antioch College and receiving a master of business administration from Harvard Business School and a grant from the Woodrow Wilson Foundation, Davis eventually embarked on a career in real-estate development. He served as the project manager for the Housing Corporation of America, where he coordinated Federal Housing Administration programs, including a 700-unit complex in Washington, D.C. Then he turned his sights to Coconut Grove, Florida.

His first development was a nine-unit town-house complex

J. S. Smolian and his grandson, Robert Davis, at Seagrove Beach in the early 1950s.

called Serendipity in an area considered inhospitable to upper-middle-income housing. Carefully arranged so as not to destroy the heavily wooded site, the two-story town houses were designed to complement the existing, low-scaled architecture of the Grove, and offered more amenities and better space planning than comparably priced units. Serendipity was both a financial and critical success, and became a model of innovative planning for other local developers.

Davis's next project was a Bauhaus- and De Stijl-inspired, ten-unit town-house complex, also in Coconut Grove, called Apogee. He built it despite warnings that no market existed for austere, three-story town houses with completely open, interconnected rooms and stained, bare concrete floors. Out of respect for the village-like ambience of the Grove, Davis sited and landscaped the town houses so that their decidedly modern profiles were not visible from the street. To promote Apogee, Davis used his own town house as a gallery for local artists, such as tropical-realist painter Jean Welch, sculptor Val Carroll, and photographer Steven Brooke. Like Serendipity, Apogee was financially successful, widely publicized, and received numerous awards, including an American Institute of Architects' Award of Excellence.

BIRTH OF AN IDEA

In 1978, more than thirty years after his first childhood visits to the Gulf Coast, Robert Davis inherited J. S. Smolian's eighty acres of "worthless sand and scrub." While contemplating his options for use of the land, he often reminisced about his idyllic summer vacations and the time his family enjoyed in the small, beachfront cottages. "When I closed my eyes and let my mind wander, I could almost feel the sea breezes evaporating the moisture on my skin. I could recall the special pleasure of relaxing on a porch rocker after a shower at the end of a day on the beach."

Inspired by his memories, Davis began with the simple notion of developing his property with wood-frame cottages similar to those of his childhood. Unpretentious and inviting, they were built of wood with deep roof overhangs, generous porches, ample windows, and cross ventilation in every room. Constructed two feet off the ground, the breezes could flow under as well as through the houses. With reasonable maintenance, these cottages lasted for generations. "They were beautifully adapted to the climate and quietly enhanced the sensual pleasure of life by the sea, where porch sitting and strolling were at least as important as swimming and sunbathing."

An unusually patient and thoughtful man, Davis allowed his ideas to evolve slowly. He studied town planning, vernacular architecture, and the histories of ancient and modern cities.

A typical Panhandle cottage.

Among his readings were articles by Leon Krier, the London-based architectural theoretician and urban designer with whom he was later to consult. (The Prince of Wales' outspoken criticism of modern architecture and his support of neoclassicism were based, in part, on Krier's theories.)

Krier writes eloquently about the restoration of the traditional city. He believes that eighty acres—the area encompassed within a quarter-mile radius—is the distance a person would comfortably walk on a daily basis to go to work, to shop, or to a café or restaurant. One might have to use mechanical transportation to go to a concert or a ball game, but not just to buy a quart of milk.

To Krier, eighty acres was the *ideal* parcel of land for a sensibly designed town, one with all of the necessities and pleasures of daily life within walking distance. After examining many development options, Davis decided to build just that: neither a conference center nor groups of cottages, but a town, his own town—the town of Seaside.

"Part of my intention," Davis explains, "was to construct a demonstrable and overdue antidote to the well-intentioned idea that took hold at the beginning of this century, the idea that social ills could be ameliorated by the separation of housing from workplaces. Certainly the desirability of living at some distance from steel mills or slaughterhouses was obvious. But this idea, like many, was distorted into the current practice of rigidly separating all land uses from each other and, thus, requiring that we spend inordinate portions of each day encapsulated in automobiles, leaving behind, at the end of the day, lifeless downtown areas. More importantly, civic intimacy was vanishing."

Vernacular cottages in DeFuniak Springs, Florida.

A cottage in DeFuniak Springs, Florida.

PLANNING THE NEW TOWN

Although Davis had been successful with his housing ventures in Miami, he was in no rush to formulate the future of his grandfather's legacy. Before deciding upon the precise architectural nature of Seaside, he and his wife, Daryl, spent two years touring the South in their 1975, red convertible Pontiac "Land Yacht," taking inventory of the architectural features that give the region's small towns their distinct character.

Daryl, Robert, and Micah Davis.

"We'd see an interesting house, knock on the door, and almost always be invited in," recalls Daryl. "The trips were a wonderful education and confirmed our desire to develop a real Florida architecture for Seaside."

"Why seal yourself up in an air-conditioned 'refrigerator,'" Davis asks, "when you live in a wonderful place with a climate that is benign most of the year?" Davis's leisurely survey convinced him to seek building types "in which you can truly enjoy the indolence of the tropics." He wanted buildings that would be comfortable even in the most humid weather. "I find it delightful to sit under a ceiling fan on a hot afternoon and just talk to passing neighbors." He was certain others would savor the experience equally.

During this period of investigation, Davis met Miami architects Andres Duany and Elizabeth Plater-Zyberk, then of the newly established firm Arquitectonica. They led Davis to think concretely about building a town designed in keeping with the native architecture.

At first Davis wanted to reinterpret the local vernacular architecture and had Arquitectonica propose several schemes. Though the firm's principals studied at Harvard, Columbia, Yale, and Princeton, they had never worked at length with anything like the Florida Panhandle's indigenous style. Their first designs—diagrammatic, cartoonlike buildings—resembled postmodern cracker houses. It seemed that nothing in the Ivy League curriculum had taught architecture students how to revive a building tradition.

"The schemes *looked* vernacular, but they were modernist in detailing," says Davis. "There were sliding-glass doors that opened into open-air pavilions; with this configuration, you lost the sense of enclosure, the feeling of a room. But I wanted rooms that felt like *rooms* and porches that felt like *porches*. In fact, the more enamored of vernacular I became, the more I wanted the design to be very straight, not reinvented or updated in any way."

In response, Duany and Plater-Zyberk began taking data-gathering journeys of their own. They traveled throughout the South, and intensively through Florida—with cameras, sketch pads, and tape measures. Eventually they and Davis felt confident about the basic rules for designing Southern vernacular, residential architecture.

The architects had been diligent about studying the buildings not in isolation, but in the context of *small towns*. They concluded that the small town *itself* was the best model for designing streets and for locating the principal elements of the community.

The result, in time, was an exhaustive compilation of fundamental architectural qualities and features. It included picket

AT LEFT:
Robert and Daryl Davis touring Grayton Beach in their 1975 Pontiac, to study the vernacular architecture of the Florida Panhandle.

fences of varying design standing approximately sixteen feet from the street; galvanized metal roofs; exteriors of wooden clapboard, board-and-batten, or shingle; screen porches with generous overhangs; and vertical window patterns with real and operable window shutters.

With this inventory in hand, Duany and Plater-Zyberk, who had by this time formed their own firm, set about developing a Building Code for Seaside. It was so literal that its effect was as liberating as it was restrictive. The Code's stipulations—covering everything from building materials to roof pitch—were so precise that they ensured the stylistic harmony of the overall development while granting great freedom to Seaside landowners as to whom they could choose to design their houses. "You could hire almost anyone to design a house here," affirms Davis, "as long as they adhered to the Code. Its compliance ensured that any building would conform to the architectural atmosphere."

In 1980, Davis finally met Leon Krier. He offered the architect-author a building plot in exchange for consultation on Seaside's Master Plan. Krier advised on such aspects as refining the pedestrian scale of the streets, ensuring that the Town Center was situated within optimum walking distance of the houses, and the siting of the recreational areas.

The fundamental concept around which Seaside was developed is that people *would* walk if walking were convenient and pleasant, and if the range of life's daily requirements were close at hand. Davis's aspiration was to create "an environment that would draw people out of their houses and onto their porches." He wanted safe streets, generous boulevards, comfortably scaled buildings, indigenous landscape, and "an atmosphere of neighborliness . . . a familiarity that promotes even the practice of cutting through backyards."

By the fall of 1980, Davis was ready to begin. He and Daryl moved permanently from cosmopolitan Miami to the Florida Gulf Coast, known locally as "The Redneck Riviera."

The first Seaside sales sign.

BUILDING THE NEW TOWN

The Red House, one of Seaside's first two houses, became the first Seaside Sales Office.

The Yellow House, Robert and Daryl Davis's first house.

Even before the Seaside Master Plan had developed far beyond the conceptual stage, Davis built his first two houses in Seaside. He felt it was important to test the marketplace to determine whether a house that *shared* the beach at the *end* of a street could be sold for a price nearly equal to that of a beachfront condominium. The conventional wisdom of the time was that this was unfeasible, and that the strict architectural controls on construction would further deter sales. The conventional wisdom was quickly proved wrong.

"It seems so easy *now* to design a building for Seaside," Davis recalls, "but it took a long time and a lot of work to develop a design for the first two houses that felt truly right. Part of the problem was Daryl and I were designing a house for ourselves that would also have to serve as the 'typical' Seaside house." While still struggling with the concept, Davis happened to glimpse a sketch of a three-bay house in Andres Duany's office. The center bay of the house had a fairly steeply pitched and gabled roof, and the side bays had a shallow-pitched hip roof. A large room was located in the center with auxiliary rooms around the perimeter. "I immediately realized that this was one of the typical house forms I had noted around the Panhandle."

Both the Red House and the Yellow House are variations on this theme. The square Red House, which became the first Seaside Sales Office, has a pyramid-shaped roof. The Yellow House, into which Robert and Daryl Davis moved, has a roof shape identical to that of the old Washaway Hotel in Grayton Beach. The roof pitches were actually measured from that older building.

By 1983, the Seaside Building Code was complete and put into practice for the first neighborhood—Tupelo Street. The Code mandated that houses had to be low and freestanding, of wood-frame

construction, and have exposed rafters, deep front porches oriented toward the prevailing warm-weather breezes, and gentle roof pitches with deep roof overhangs. The cottages were to be built off the ground, to allow air to circulate under them; in short, they were to be naturally ventilated, passive solar houses.

The Code also required that houses be painted in pastel colors with approved contrasting trim. Windows had to be square or vertical; shutters had to be real and operable; roofs had to be metal or wood shake. Landscaping of the mandatory yards had to be of sand and native scrub, not grass. Each house had to have its own white picket fence, with no pattern repeated on any one street.

To demonstrate Seaside's commitment to the public domain, a Gazebo was built at the end of the first block on Tupelo Street. Visible from the main county road, this graceful and unpretentious structure in large measure established the scale of Seaside's first street.

Shortly thereafter, the Tupelo Street Beach Pavilion was built as a symbolic gateway to the sea, an invitation to *share* the beach—a stark contrast to the high-rise condominiums that block the view and access to the sea. The Tupelo Street Beach Pavilion became not just an icon for Seaside but also a widely used symbol for Florida's remaining unspoiled beaches and the growing commitment to preserve them.

These simple landmark structures (usually absent from most planned developments, except, perhaps, for a solitary guardhouse) transformed Tupelo Street—with less than a dozen houses—into a real neighborhood, and made it possible to perceive at a glance the basic urban concept of Seaside.

Initial sales in 1982 were better than anticipated, helped by an early recognition in both the architectural and popular press that the Seaside plan might very well become a model for changing the patterns of urban and suburban growth.

AT LEFT:
Early Tupelo Street with the Tupelo Street Beach Pavilion. Even with so few structures, the planning behind Seaside was evident.

The Tupelo Street Gazebo with the Tupelo Street Beach Pavilion in the background.

THE INFLUENCE OF SEASIDE

In an unprecedentedly short period of time, Seaside changed thinking about neighborhoods, towns, and civic history. Architects, designers, planners, as well as nonprofessionals began visiting in increasing numbers. Some who were skeptical had been openly critical of what they anticipated would be a cute, self-conscious, Disneyland-like environment. The look of the embellished, pastel-colored, Victorian-inspired cottages of the much-publicized Rosewalk section may have perpetuated this impression in the press; in person, most visitors came away with a different feel.

Unlike Disneyland, Seaside is made of real, indigenous materials with no pretence as to what they are. "When these materials and forms were criticized as being nostalgic," Davis points out, "it was because too many people had lost touch with the vernacular tradition, and had difficulty distinguishing between the artificial and the real."

The exuberant design of some Seaside cottages is also a genuine expression of the vernacular building tradition, and quite appropriate to a relaxed, less restrained summer place dedicated to celebration and fantasy. One of the models for Seaside was the colorful Oak Bluffs in Martha's Vineyard. It, too, is constructed of indigenous materials that express its own local building tradition. Davis notes that ". . . the murals in the houses of Pompeii were no doubt more exuberant than those back home in Rome; and it is safe to say that the summer houses of Brighton and Bath are more buoyant than the permanent residences of Georgian London."

In time, it was generally acknowledged that Seaside is less about pastel cottages than it is about the dedicated practice of humane design and planning principles. The unambiguous logic of the *overall* Seaside Plan—the pedestrian-scaled and well-proportioned streets, the accessible beach pavilions, the harmonious grouping of residential and commercial buildings, the absence of high-rise beachside condos—makes a persuasive case for Seaside's underlying message: civilized liveability.

Seaside's porches and picket fences promote conversations and contribute to its inherent neighborliness.

PUBLIC AND PROFESSIONAL ACCLAIM

"I believe that the lessons they're working out at Seaside have very serious applications, both in rural areas and in our cities," wrote His Royal Highness, the Prince of Wales, in *A Vision of Britain: A Personal View of Architecture.*

In 1983, after less than two years of development, Seaside's Town Plan received an Award of Excellence from the South Florida Chapter of the American Institute of Architects (AIA) and, in 1984, from the Florida Chapter of the AIA. Also in 1984, *Progressive Architecture* awarded its Town Plan a Citation of Merit.

In 1986, with the town less than five years old, Seaside won both the Florida Governor's Design Award and *Builder Magazine*'s Grand Award. Also in 1986, the Connecticut Society of Architects gave the Rosewalk, designed by architects Robert Orr and Melanie Taylor, an Award of Excellence.

In 1987, *Progressive Architecture* again honored Seaside with a Citation for the Hybrid Building, now called Dreamland Heights, designed by architect Steven Holl. The American Wood Council gave Merit Awards in its nonresidential category to the PER-SPI-CAS-ITY Market, designed by architect Deborah Berke, and the Ruskin Street Beach Pavilion, designed by architects Stuart Cohen and Anders Nereim.

In 1988, Seaside received the coveted AIA's National Citation Award for Excellence in Urban Design in addition to the Southeast Builders' Conference Grand Award and the Florida AIA Citation for Excellence in Urban Design. Also, the PER-SPI-CAS-ITY Market received an award from *Builder Magazine.*

In 1989, Seaside received, among other awards, a Southern Living Home Award, a Progressive Architecture Award, Builder Magazine Grand Awards for the Krier Cottage, designed by architect Leon Krier, and for the Honeymoon Cottages, designed by architect Scott Merrill, and a Merit Award for architect Walter Chatham's East Ruskin Street House.

Seaside's fame soon spread beyond the architecture and design community. It was clear that the town was far more than an academic study; it was a tangible example of the success of building principles based upon human scale and activity. This message was not lost on the general public, which visited in record numbers. Unlike many fashionable developments, Seaside drew buyers principally from neighboring regions; others came from as far as Sweden.

Articles about "The New Town with the Old Ways" appeared in literally hundreds of newspapers, magazines, journals, and books around the world. Here is a sampling of the praise Seaside garnered there:

From Robert Campbell of *The Boston Globe*: "[Seaside is] perhaps the most important new piece of architecture in the country. [It] teaches us that there is another kind of growth—growth that occurs in concentrated, walkable settlements instead of an endlessly dispersed sprawl."

From Robert Sertl of *Travel & Leisure*: "Seaside in Florida has revived an old idea. . . . It contains the seeds of a land-development philosophy that could influence the way America lives in the 21st century."

From Tom Fisher of *Progressive Architecture*: "Seaside is providing a whole new basis for zoning in this country."

From *Smithsonian Magazine*: "Seaside is an experiment not just in planning and design, but in living."

From *Architectural Record*: "It is one thing to replicate the physical features of a small Southern town, quite another to recapture a vanishing way of life. Developer Robert Davis has tried to do both. . . ."

From *The Atlantic Monthly*: ". . . Seaside has become the most celebrated new American town of the decade."

In 1990, Seaside was acclaimed for both its planning and its individual buildings. On New Year's Day, *Time* magazine selected Seaside as one of its "Designs of the Decade," along with such contemporary icons of American design as Maya Ying Lin's Vietnam Memorial and the Apple Macintosh Computer.

At the 1990 National AIA Honor Awards Convention in Washington, D.C., Seaside received an unprecedented four awards. The Town of Seaside was honored for its "significant contribution to the architectural profession." National Honor Awards were given to Scott Merrill for his Honeymoon Cottages, to Walter Chatham for his East Ruskin Street House, and to Steven Holl for Dreamland Heights. Seaside also received the Florida Department of Natural Resources Award.

Seaside in 1986. Houses were yet to be built on the west side of the Town Center.

The "Seaside Skyline" in 1984.

Seaside in 1992.

24

THE LEGACY OF SEASIDE

Throughout the world, in lectures to architects; planners; developers; zoning boards; traffic engineers; and city, state, and government officials of all ranks—literally, to whomever will listen—Andres Duany and Elizabeth Plater-Zyberk champion what the *Woodrow Wilson Quarterly* appropriately called "The Second Coming of the American Small Town." The *Quarterly*'s Winter 1992 edition cited the architects for ". . . calling for a return to the human and communal elegance of the small town." Recognizing that this work has implications far beyond town planning, the *Quarterly* praised them for imploring all of us to be "concerned with . . . regaining control of our communal existence, which, among other things, is the first step toward addressing national and even global problems."

Duany and Plater-Zyberk have applied the planning principles they developed at Seaside to more than eighty new town and urban revitalization projects to date. Among these are a 100-acre development of houses, offices, and shops south of Manchester, New Hampshire; a 550-acre town southwest of Austin, Texas; and a 3,500-acre site in Blount Springs, north of Birmingham, Alabama.

They established a master's program in urban planning at the University of Miami and are directly involved in the programs for rebuilding and redesigning Miami neighborhoods destroyed by Hurricane Andrew. Through an ongoing series of intense, community-wide discussion and planning sessions (called "charrettes") they encourage others to study and apply humane urban-design principles to the rebuilding of their neighborhoods.

One such project is the South Miami Heights Community Center and Caribbean School Study, led by Miami architect Suzanne Martinson. This study proposes to rebuild the Caribbean Elementary School as a "full-service" school, incorporating a health-care facility, an early-childhood center, and adult-education classrooms.

Owners of the larger properties adjacent to the school expressed their willingness to cooperate with local residents to build a neighborhood Community Center with space for Community Development Corporation offices, public parks, public services, and low-density housing. The model for the full-service school received national attention and was presented to the secretary of education. The neighborhood has formed its own Community Development Corporation to oversee the progress. There is community-wide optimism that the plan can succeed. The very fact that projects such as these exist is testament to Seaside's influence and inspiration.

Today, Andres Duany's compilation of detailed fundamental elements, guidelines, and schematics for Traditional Neighborhood Development, Land Planning, and Site Development has

been incorporated into the *Architectural Graphic Standards*, the industry's widely distributed compendium of building details and standards.

Traditional Neighborhood Development principles are presented in the *Architectural Graphic Standards* not as academic theory, but as proven guidelines that demonstrate the forms of land use that create successful neighborhoods and promote a balanced mix of human activity, rather than, in Duany's words, ". . . congested, fragmented, unsatisfying, suburban sprawl." The body of information that Seaside generated is now available to a vast spectrum of practitioners, and particularly to those greatest in need, i.e., our city planning and zoning departments.

SEASIDE AND THE IDEAL CITY

Robert Davis readily admits that "Seaside is . . . an idealized vision of a town, and . . . as a holiday town . . . does not contain a full complement of human activities." Though Seaside will eventually have a school, and the Ruskin Place residential/workshop district is progressing rapidly, it comprises no factories or industries, nor is there room for any. Davis also points out that "Seaside's success as a holiday town means that daily and weekly rentals are more profitable than annual leases; thus the garage apartments, apartments above the stores, and other smaller building types which, in other circumstances, might provide affordable housing for workers, instead provide less expensive accommodations for vacationers."

The town's limitations notwithstanding, Davis believes: "Its

AT LEFT:
An aerial shot of Seaside taken in November 1992.

idealized vision can be translated to 'real' cities. And the compromises necessary in the translation will likely produce a result which, in the end, is more satisfactory than the 'ideal.'"

During his fellowship at the American Academy in Rome in 1991, he set out to study the realization of the planning principles of the *città ideale*—the Ideal City—those cities literally planned from the ground up. He examined Italy's planned towns, including those of the Renaissance (such as Pienza and Castlefranco) and the Fascist new towns and quarters of the 1930s (such as Pontinia and Rome's Garbatella district).

During the course of his travels he concluded: ". . . The more fully realized examples of 'ideal cities,' like Sabbionetta and Palmanova, were far less interesting than places like Pienza where existing reality forced a series of compromises that made the end

Walking along Seaside Avenue.

result more liveable and even more beautiful. In that sense, Rome, itself, is the ideal city. It is a place where the ambitious plans of the Renaissance popes fell victim to their generally short reigns and their limited resources, at least in comparison to those of 17th-century French kings or 19th-century French emperors. But the achievements of the Renaissance popes are nonetheless quite wonderful, and they impart a legibility to Rome that it would not otherwise have. Those radiating avenues with vistas terminated by obelisks have become integrated, in turn, into the almost magical context of a town with 2,500 years of urban and architectural history layered one upon the other."

Davis continues, "The ideal city does not have to be a perfect realization of the *Città Ideale.* This understanding provides an incentive to undertake the financial and political risks involved in a project's partial realization, and to incorporate some of these ideas into our plans for the future, always looking carefully at existing reality to see what works."

With all due respect to the professional and civic accolades, it is the relaxed community atmosphere that proves how successfully Seaside does work. It has managed to revive the notion of public life in late-twentieth-century America and is stimulating the recovery of earlier American urban history. It represents the essence of community. The cars stay parked and residents stroll; neighbors know one another; all age groups mix freely; and single-family houses coexist with town houses and shops. In view of the past fifty years of urban development in America, this is no small accomplishment.

One of the many festivals held in the Seaside Town Center Amphitheater.

THE SEASIDE CODE

The Master Plan and Seaside Urban Code were drafted in the summer of 1982. While they continually evolve, they are still based upon their original simple, cogent concepts. Both the Plan and Code are graphic documents, easily understood by the citizen-buyer.

As few rules as necessary are incorporated into the Code in order to ensure that each Seaside house will continue the regional building tradition and will contribute to giving Seaside's neighborhoods the cohesion and strong sense of place that characterize such American towns as Charleston, Savannah, Nantucket, and Cape May. Seaside's houses share a common vocabulary of building forms and materials, but great variety and heterogeneity exist and are encouraged.

The Code, which reads like an outline for a nineteenth-century town, is coordinated with the Master Plan to produce streets that are physically comfortable and visually delightful for pedestrians. Although they are designed to accommodate cars and parking, they also encourage walking over driving.

The guidelines are explicit enough to allow purchasers who do not wish to hire architects to work directly with contractors and builders.

In Seaside's early years, Davis enforced the Code virtually single-handedly and presided over nearly every aspect of the town's development, from the stationery type styles to the entrées for the restaurant. Architects working at Seaside often referred to Davis as "the duke." It is, in fact, his sweeping personal commitment that facilitates the quality control unique in a speculative project of this type.

Many architects have found the Seaside Code restrictive. Some prominent designers tried unsuccessfully to circumvent its constraints, and their designs were rejected. Others simply refused even to attempt to design within its rules. New York architect Deborah Berke, on the other hand, who has an outspoken disdain for architectural melodrama, found room enough in the Code to produce more than a dozen elegant and unembellished, yet stylistically distinctive houses. Designs by architects Walter Chatham, Rafael Pelli, Alex Gorlin, Victoria Casasco, and Carey McWhorter all demonstrate the real flexibility inherent in the Code. These houses are featured in "A Walk Through Seaside," later in this book.

Homeowners and their builder confer on construction of their new house.

URBAN CODE · THE TOWN OF SEASIDE

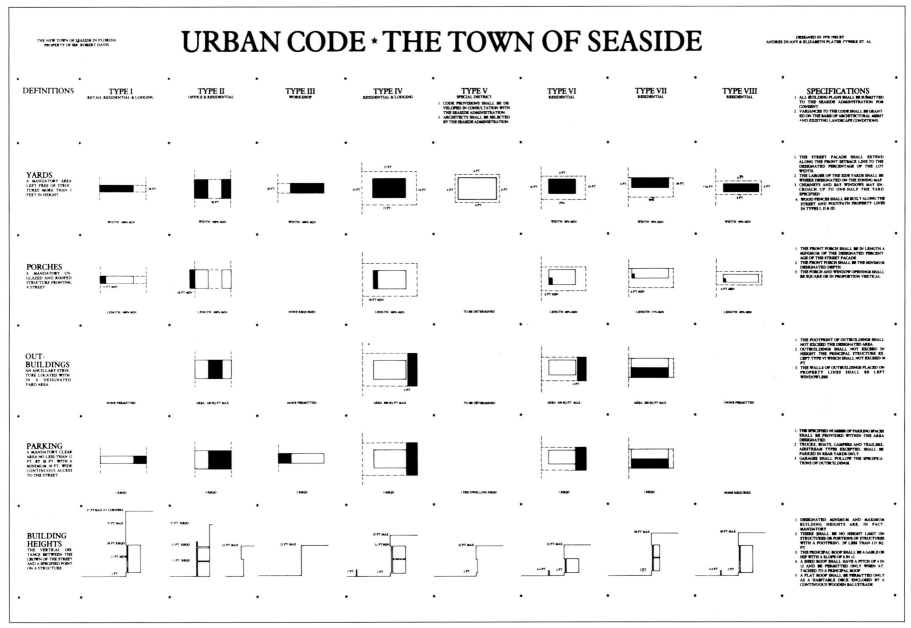

The Seaside Code spells out the required aspects of building form.

31

ELEMENTS OF THE SEASIDE VERNACULAR

Seaside is actually a synthesis of many vernacular traditions ranging from the Victorian and Carpenter Gothic to those of Charleston and the antebellum South. Also, as the Dreamland Heights Hybrid Building and several Ruskin Place town houses demonstrate, it comfortably accommodates aspects of modernist design. These traditions are expressed in the building elements—picket fences, porches, towers, roofs, and windows—as well as in the varied use of the prescribed building materials.

Picket fences add visual interest to streets and pathways.

Picket Fences

Picket fences were required not only for their evocative appeal, but also because they serve the critical role of defining the edge and maintaining the scale of the street. In Duany and Plater-Zyberk's words, "... [they] project the human presence within the house to those passing on the street." The effect, ultimately, encourages pedestrian traffic.

Seaside's white picket fences are true vernacular forms and are as individual as regional accents in speech. This expression of background and taste prevents the dulling homogeneity of overly planned developments such as those in Boca Raton, Florida, or Miami's Fisher Island. These projects, unlike Seaside, are usually the result of one designer using the same motifs with numbing regularity and no authentic variety.

With the exception of the larger-scaled Town Center buildings and the Lyceum, the Code requires white painted, wood picket fences at the street-front and path-front property lines. Seaside Avenue lots require picket fences at the front setback lines. Individual fence patterns may not replicate each other on the same street. A gateway and entrance from all streets and footpaths must be provided.

Picket fences along Savannah Street.

Porches

Every house at Seaside is required to have a front porch. The distance from the front porch to the picket fence was calculated to accommodate neighborly chats. While picket fences promote short exchanges, porches encourage longer conversations. They are a gentle transition between the completely private life within and the public life of the street. Even intensely private people have shown surprising gregariousness under the spell of a front porch.

Many Seaside cottages also have side and back porches. These offer the advantages of ventilation and contact with the sights, sounds, and smells of the environment but with more privacy than a front porch. While the front porch offers an inviting site for afternoon tea, a side porch facing an inner courtyard is ideal for a midday nap or an intimate dinner.

AT LEFT:
Watching the sunset from the porch of Josephine's Bed & Breakfast.

AT RIGHT:
The porch of the Dreamsicle Cottage, designed by Orr and Taylor.

Towers

From Rapunzel's storybook dwelling to Hilda's Dovecote in Hawthorne's *Marble Faun,* and from the stone fortresses of San Gimignano to the lighthouses of sea fables, towers have been quintessential symbols of mystery and romance. They are also among Seaside's most recognizable features, contributing to the charm of the skyline and affording even the most "landlocked" homeowners a sea view.

The first example of what could be accomplished with this form was the tower on 109 Tupelo Street, designed by Deborah Berke. Since then, towers have been used as small studios, additional bedrooms, and simply as cozy places to string up a hammock. The views from Seaside's towers are always magnificent and "tower parties" are uniquely enjoyable. For many, the tower provides a private retreat, a solitary place to reflect, read a book, write a letter, or watch the sunset. Some homeowners have claimed it to be their "single favorite place on Earth."

Seaside's towers are among its most dramatic features.

The tower of the House of the Mathematician in Dreamland Heights.

Seaside's first tower, at 109 Tupelo Street, designed by Deborah Berke.

AT RIGHT:
The view from the tower of the Krier Cottage, 115 Tupelo Street, designed by Leon Krier.

Roofs

The profile of a roof is among the most defining characteristics of a house. The peaked roof, for example, appears almost universally in children's drawings of "a house." The Code carefully specifies rooflines and roof details typical of the Gulf region. The high-pitched roof (eight in twelve) with deep overhangs was chosen for the ventilation and sun protection it affords and for its ease of waterproofing as much as for aesthetics.

In keeping with traditional design, Seaside roofs must have symmetrical peaks and soffits are not permitted. Fascias may not completely cover rafter tails, and roof cladding materials must be either wood shake, metal shingle, corrugated metal sheet, *V*-crimp metal sheet, or standing seam metal sheet. Metal roofs may not be painted. Flat roofs are permitted only when accessible from an adjacent enclosed space.

In keeping with the local vernacular, one of the first houses built at Seaside was given a tin roof. Tin roofs are easy to fabricate and are highly affordable. Some area residents who thought the material "cheap looking" wrote bitter (even threatening) complaints to Davis that he was making the community look like "Tobacco Road."

Local developers predicted the choice was a guarantee of his failure. This initial resistance only further proved to Davis how far designers, planners, and local residents had distanced themselves from their own local building traditions—which, in fact, *did* include tin roofs.

One of the early Seaside houses used shake shingles on its roof. They did not age as well near the beach, however, and, even though permitted by the Code, were not selected by other homeowners who, despite the early controversy, tended to use tin.

Peaked tin roofs, one of the traditional vernacular features of Seaside architecture.

Detail of the rafters of the Krier Cottage.

116 East Ruskin Street, Walter Chatham.

Windows

Like the roofline, windows contribute significantly to the overall character of both the individual house and the neighborhood. Vertical windows subtly echo the standing human form and small square windows mirror the human face.

Vertical window forms found throughout the country contrast sharply with the large, unsegmented, horizontal or "picture" windows typical of postwar ranch houses. Some design theorists have criticized picture windows as defeating the very notion of shelter and reducing views of the landscape to a large, static mural or TV screen. In his book *Architectural Compositions*, Rob Krier writes, "Our awareness of the outside world is intensified by . . . windows with structuring bars . . . and becomes weaker the bigger the window opening is." (Leonardo da Vinci himself advises that small rooms strengthen the mind while larger ones weaken it.)

The Seaside Code specifies the traditional window types that harmoniously work with the other vernacular elements. Windows are specified as casement, awning, or double hung. Individual windows and porch openings must be square or, when rectangular, of a vertical proportion not less than 1:1.5. They are required to be constructed of wood, or wood with metal or plastic cladding. Only true divided lights are permitted rather than the very common, artificial "snap-ins." Shutters, too, must be real and operable. Horizontal awning-type windows are allowed only at clerestories.

Windows are considered so important to the overall ambience and scale of Seaside that proposals for any other window types—fan windows, circle windows, stained glass, or fixed glass—must be submitted for approval to the Seaside Architectural Review Committee to ensure their compatibility.

The vertical or square window typical of houses in most Southern towns is required at Seaside.

Examples of vertical windows. Large, horizontal "picture windows" are not permitted.

Materials

Too often, buildings today are constructed without thought or concern as to how the building materials will age, what kind of maintenance they will require, or what excessive expenditures of energy will be necessary to keep the buildings comfortable.

The deterioration of many inner-city urban projects, carelessly designed and built with lowest-bidder construction techniques, has bred a public cynicism that threatens to kill community spirit and make further progress even more difficult, if not impossible. The deterioration of such prominent buildings as the Fine Arts Center of the University of Massachusetts should remind us that materials must be appropriate to a particular climate and designs must take into account the limitations of those materials.

The materials mandated for Seaside buildings are selected for honesty in function and their ability to age gracefully. All wood exposed to weather, for example, must be of cedar, redwood, cypress, or pressure-treated pine. Nontreated pine may be used *only* when properly finished to prevent moisture from rotting the wood. Chimneys must be masonry, brick, or sheet metal; no wood chases or enclosures are permitted.

Materials are chosen for their functional honesty and ability to age gracefully.

AT LEFT:
The Dreamland Heights uses many common materials in expressive ways.

Stained wood exteriors age well in the North Florida climate.

Architect Deborah Berke used unpainted, corrugated tin for the exterior of the Seaside Meeting Hall, giving the building a frontier-town quality.

AT LEFT:
The Natchez Street Beach Pavilion, designed by the Jersey Devils—architects Steve Badanes and Jim Adamson—was constructed as carefully as fine furniture.

43

Footpaths

Dirt footpaths throughout Seaside provide additional networks for pedestrian traffic. They also provide unexpected vistas and intimate views of Seaside houses and gardens. Children love using them as private highways.

Footpaths connect Rosewalk cottages.

Footpaths were designed as part of the initial Seaside plan.

AT RIGHT:
Footpaths run the full length of the beach.

Gardens

Except for the Town Center, there are no lawns at Seaside. This eliminates the need for fertilizers, excess water, and constant maintenance (noisy mowers are not welcome). The Code prohibits lawns and specifies that all vegetation must be native, purposely excluding exotic species which, in other areas, have overtaken the natives. Not surprisingly, native materials are wonderfully compatible with the vernacular architecture and well adapted to the strenuous North Florida seacoast climate with its salt, wind, cold, and pests. Exotics are unwelcome also because local birds do not recognize (or like) them, which inhibits natural reseeding.

Early in Seaside's development, landscape architect Douglas Duany was commissioned to design the town landscape. He strongly emphasized use of native species. Working with him were landscapers Clark and Charlotte Thompson, who moved to the Panhandle from Lake Tahoe. Since then, the Thompsons have developed landscape plans for many Seaside houses.

They discovered that while most people attracted to Seaside are not interested in clear cutting the vegetation, they are unfamiliar with the native vegetation and tend to think of it merely as scrub. The Thompsons have made it part of their business to educate new homeowners about what *not* to remove and which native species to substitute for the exotic, more flamboyant flowers many of them originally wanted. Among their more popular recommendations are beautiful yet hardy species such as oaks, magnolias, wax myrtle, and yaupons. They also recommend species that do not require constant irrigation after the delicate first year of planting.

Each cottage offers the opportunity to express the character of the site and the personality of the owners, and the gardens are as individual as the homeowners themselves. Landscape styles range from the wild and uninhibited, to the precise and sculptural. The interweaving of the different local vines and flowers with the picket fences creates additional visual variety.

All landscape materials used in Seaside are native species.

A cottage using coco palms as its main landscape feature.

AT RIGHT:
The various native ground covers and bushes create a rich texture.

For the "Dune House," located on the beach and practically buried in brush, Charlotte Thompson recalls, "It was most important to first uphold the character of the dune and then unobtrusively sculpt the bordering vegetation. It is simply not practical to keep a flower garden in an area of this rough character."

It took until 1995 for Seaside's first streets—Tupelo and Savannah—to begin maturing. The Thompsons look toward the full maturity of Seaside's landscape by about 2005.

Beauty-berry.

Pampas grass.

AT LEFT:
Woody goldenrod attracts monarch butterflies.

Endangered sea oats are cultivated along the dunes.

Pittosporum and verbena.

Yaupon.

Sumac (nonpoisonous) planted along Sea-side Avenue.

Loblolly pines along Forest Street.

Beach sunflower.

Pentas.

HOUSE AND BUILDING TYPES

The Seaside Code defines eight specific building types and their particular space requirements.

Type I

These lots define the large Central Square that runs along County Route C-30A. The zoning is intended for retail on the ground floors and residential above. Type I buildings are Seaside's tallest at a maximum of five stories in height. They have party walls with no front setbacks, and they require a large arcade. Their prototype is found on main streets throughout the South. One such example is the Charleston Battery.

Type II

These lots define the small pedestrian square at the front of the town hall. Zoning is intended primarily for office use, although there is provision for apartments and retail establishments. The Code dictates four-story buildings with courtyards and smaller buildings at the rear. Only minimum variety in arcades and silhouettes is allowed. This square is intended to have a decidedly more sedate and dignified appearance than the Central Square. Its prototype is found in the Vieux Carré of New Orleans.

The Lyceum, designed by Walter Chatham, is a Type II building.

AT LEFT:
*The Modica Market, designed by Deborah Berke,
and Dreamland Heights, designed by Steven Holl,
are examples of a Type I building.*

51

Type III

These buildings have two uses, which are ultimately determined by lot size and location. Large lots face the service street at the rear of the Central Square. Warehouses for storage and workshops will occupy them. Small lots occur along the north-south pedestrian route and connect what will be the church with the Central Square. These are for small shops. Type III buildings are party-wall buildings with few restrictions other than a limit on height. Their prototype is Jackson Square in New Orleans.

Type IV

These are the large lots that line Seaside Avenue, which connects the Central Square to the tennis and pool areas. Type IV buildings are large, freestanding buildings with substantial outbuildings at the rear. This type includes private houses, small apartment buildings, or bed-and-breakfast inns. The setbacks on all sides, together with a continuous porch mandated for the street front, generate a look of grandeur. Their prototype is the Greek Revival mansion of the antebellum South.

The town houses at Ruskin Place, Type III buildings.

203 Seaside Avenue, designed by architect Don Cooper, is a Type IV building.

Type V

This is a special category for large lots that can contain several buildings. The lots must be planned as coherent groupings.

The Honeymoon Cottages, designed by architect Scott Merrill, are Type V buildings.

Type VI

These lots constitute the suburban section of Seaside. They occur on the north-south streets with views of the sea. Lots become slightly smaller toward the center to promote increased density. Type VI buildings are freestanding houses for which the construction of small outbuildings at the rear for use as guesthouses and rental units are encouraged. Requirements for substantial-sized front yards secure the view of the sea for inland units. The picket fences help to maintain the street edge. The prototype is found throughout the suburban and rural South.

101 Savannah Street, designed by architect Deborah Berke, is a Type VI building.

A view along the beach at sunset.

Type VII

This building type occurs along the east-west streets where no view of the sea is possible. Lots are smaller and less expensive. Since a view corridor is unnecessary, the front setbacks are minimal. A zero setback is permitted along one of the side yards. The Type VII prototype is the Charleston single house with a side yard.

103 Grayton, designed by Scott Merrill, is a Type VII building.

AT RIGHT:
The Krier Cottage, designed by theorist-architect Leon Krier at 115 Tupelo Street, is a Type VIII building.

Type VIII

These buildings are found throughout the residential areas of town on sites that function as gateways or focal points. The Code provisions are more liberal than those of Type VI and Type VII, permitting slightly greater height and freedom of placement on the lot. This flexibility allows for greater variety within the residential districts.

A WALK THROUGH SEASIDE

"A Walk Through Seaside" consists of five separate walks, each of which concentrates on a particular section of the town. The walks are arranged in approximate chronological order. Walks #1 and #2 guide you through Seaside's oldest sections; Walks #3, #4, and #5, through its newest. Although each walk suggests a particular sequence of streets, feel free to take detours along the footpaths that interconnect the streets.

The East Side

WALK #1: EAST ALONG THE BEACH FOOTPATH

*From the Town Center, cross C-30A, turn left onto the beach footpath,
and follow it east.*

The Honeymoon Cottages

Designed by architect Scott Merrill, who was at one time Seaside's town architect, the Honeymoon Cottages are modelled on Thomas Jefferson's Cottage at Monticello, a small outbuilding where he lived while working on Monticello. These two-story cottages, beautifully set into the dunes, are a finely crafted yet unpretentious hideaway.

They were awarded a National American Institute of Architects Award of Excellence. The jury noted, "These superb two-story beach cottages . . . evoke the coastal architecture of the area without indulging in cliches. Demonstrating a masterful use of wood construction, the architect has created cottages that are at once familiar yet fresh."

The Honeymoon Cottages, designed by Scott Merrill.

View from the porch of a Honeymoon Cottage.

A Honeymoon Cottage bedroom.

Continue east along the footpath.

Continue east along the footpath.

The East Ruskin Street Beach Pavilion

Designed by architects Stuart Cohen and Anders Nereim, this pavilion explores the idea of integrating architecture and furniture. The extensive latticework you see here is a motif repeated throughout Seaside.

54 Savannah Street (on C-30A); Designed by architect John Massengale

52 Savannah Street (on C-30A); Designed by architect Tom Christ

51 Savannah Street (on C-30A); Designed by Tom Christ

The Savannah Street Beach Pavilion

Designed by Tom Christ, this pavilion's quiet, monumental presence was created with a minimum of structural elements. Its graceful stairway was the first to provide a grand procession to the beach, and has been an influence on other pavilion designers.

54 Tupelo Street (on C-30A); Designed by Scott Merrill
53 Tupelo (on C-30A); Designed by architect Don Cooper
52 Tupelo (on C-30A); Designed by Scott Merrill

The Tupelo Street Beach Pavilion

The Tupelo Street Beach Pavilion, one of the most photographed buildings in Seaside, was designed by architect Ernesto Buch. The pavilion's arch is used as Seaside's logo, and can be found on stationery, posters, menus, and announcements.

54 Tupelo Street.

AT RIGHT:
Tupelo Street Beach Pavilion at sunset, designed by Ernesto Buch.

The Tupelo Street Beach Pavilion from the beach side.

WALK #2: EAST SIDE RESIDENTIAL

Cross C-30A and begin your walk north on Tupelo Street,
Seaside's first street.

Tupelo Street

Tupelo Street was the first street to be developed at Seaside. It contains all the elements of a beautiful street: trees and picket fences to provide a sense of containment; narrow streets paved with brick to encourage foot traffic; houses of scale comparable to one another and the width of the street; and a gazebo to mark the end of the block.

101 Tupelo Street; Designed by Tom Christ
102 Tupelo Street; Designed by Ernesto Buch
103 Tupelo Street, The Red House
Designed by Robert Davis, this cottage was used as Seaside's first Sales Office.

103 Tupelo.

104 Tupelo Street
Designed by architect Deborah Berke, this simple, straightforward cottage is beautifully proportioned and was a model for other Seaside architects.
105 Tupelo Street, The Yellow House; Designed by Robert Davis
106 Tupelo Street; Designed by architect Vic Bowman
107 Tupelo Street; Designed by architect Melanie Taylor
109 Tupelo Street, Giant's Roost and Tower
Designed by Deborah Berke, Seaside's first tower was built in 1983 as a tiny retreat for a family of four. It has two bedrooms, one and one-half baths, a screened-porch living room, and an open-air viewing deck on the top floor. The main house was built later, but for several years this twelve-foot-wide tower functioned as the cottage.
110 Tupelo Street; Designed by architect Derrick Smith

AT RIGHT:
109 Tupelo.

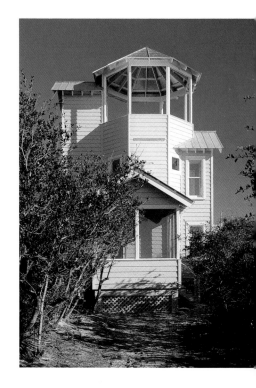

AT LEFT:
104 Tupelo.

At the gateway between 107 and 109 Tupelo Street, turn right into the Rosewalk. At the footpath, look to the left to see the steps by which you will leave Rosewalk and return to Tupelo Street. But first, walk the footpaths and explore this Victorian-inspired section of Seaside.

The Rosewalk

Designed by architects Melanie Taylor and Robert Orr, the Rosewalk was among the first group of houses built at Seaside and contains the first two-story structures. A compound of fourteen small cottages, it is centered on a garden court. Many of Rosewalk's architectural and decorative details are repeated throughout Seaside.

The Rosewalk Cottages.

129 Rosewalk, The Dreamsicle Cottage; Interior designed by Daryl Davis

Rosewalk Cottages designed by Orr and Taylor:
124 Rosewalk
122 and 123 Rosewalk
120 Rosewalk

124 Rosewalk.

Leave the main group of Rosewalk Cottages by the steps; at the end of the path you will come to 117 Rosewalk.

117 Rosewalk, Treetops Cottage; Interior designed by architect Sarah Blanch

Walk along the footpath until you come to Grove Avenue. Turn left and return to Tupelo Street.

The Tupelo Street Gazebo

Designed by Tom Christ, the Tupelo Street Gazebo is an example of how even a modest monument enhances the scale and adds focus to a street. The Gazebo is a favorite site for weddings, street parties, souvenir photographs, and fashion and catalogue sessions.

115 Tupelo Street, the Krier Cottage, and a view of the Tupelo Circle and Gazebo.

115 Tupelo Street, Krier Cottage

After years as a "paper architect," Leon Krier saw his first built project realized in Seaside. "I always said I would never build unless the conditions were right; Seaside was a dream come true."

This one-bedroom, two-bath cottage was conceived as a gate to the eastern entry to Seaside. Situated on the highest point in the town, its rooftop studio/temple projects above the live oaks and serves as a landmark.

Krier provided simple, yet precise sketches of the architectural details to Louisiana contractor Benoit Laurent, who built the cottage without supervision and with only twelve telephone calls from Krier.

The Krier Cottage is inspired by the Greek Revival style. It has only one room per floor, making the relatively small house appear tall and "modestly monumental." The bedroom is located on the lowest level, the living room on the second, and the studio/temple on the top floor. The temple contains a library that has views in three directions.

Each of the loggias and porches is treated differently. The loggia off the first-floor sitting room is built as a framed porch with access to the grounds via a short stair. Each of the other loggia/porches has a roof supported by columns of different orders, modified from Greek architecture or from Krier's own design. The entry-porch roof on the north evokes the Doric order. The balcony loggia on the west side of the living room resembles the Ionic. The studio balcony columns are classically inspired.

Krier's original choice of color was "barn red," a color he conceived of using while he was still in London with its grey skies. After considering the effect of this color—"a big fire station"—he chose an elegant creamy white that changes according to the quality of light.

A joining of classical proportions and local woodworkers' craft, the Krier Cottage is an excellent example of what can be accomplished with traditional materials and techniques.

The third-floor temple projects above the trees and serves as an eastern landmark.

The porch of the Krier Cottage.

AT RIGHT:
The view from the third-floor tower.

111 Tupelo Street; Designed by Vic Bowman
112 Tupelo Street; Designed by architect Warren Gresham
114 Tupelo Street; Designed by Tom Christ
116 Tupelo Street; Designed by Don Cooper
201 Tupelo Street; Designed by Ernesto Buch
202 Tupelo Street; Designed by Ernesto Buch/Teofilio Victoria
205 Tupelo Street; Designed by Robert Davis
206 Tupelo Street; Designed by architects Crawford/Mc-Williams/Hatcher

Continue north on Tupelo Street.

207 Tupelo Street
Designed by Deborah Berke, this cottage is an interpretation of the Southern "shotgun house." The long, narrow lot afforded Gulf views only from the front and the rear. The cottage was elongated to include both locations. The main part of the cottage, set at the back of the lot, is connected to the second floor of the entry tower by a bridge that functions as a sun deck.

207 Tupelo (on left).

74

208 Tupelo Street; Designed by Tom Christ
209 Tupelo Street; Designed by Tom Christ
210 Tupelo Street; Designed by Tom Christ
211 Tupelo Street; Designed by Ernesto Buch

212 Tupelo Street; Designed by Walter Chatham
213 Tupelo Street; Designed by Derrick Smith
214 Tupelo Street; Designed by Peter Horn

210 Tupelo.

At the end of Tupelo Street, cross Forest Street to see the Public Works Buildings.

The Public Works Buildings

The Department of Public Works was designed by Ernesto Buch; the Tower Building by Tom Christ. Reminiscent of nineteenth-century railroad sheds, these buildings incorporate maintenance facilities and administrative offices. They demonstrate innovative uses of common building materials.

Public Works Buildings; the Tower was designed by Tom Christ.

The Department of Public Works, designed by Ernesto Buch.

Continue west on Forest Street until you reach Savannah Street. Turn left and head south on Savannah Street to the next group of cottages.

Savannah Street

205 Savannah.

Guest Cottage of 120 Savannah.

209 Savannah Street; Designed by architect Larry Taylor

207 Savannah Street; Designed by Tom Christ

206 Savannah Street; Designed by Deborah Berke

205 Savannah Street; Designed by Deborah Berke

204 Savannah Street; Designed by Aubrey Garrison

203 Savannah Street; Designed by Deborah Berke

120 Savannah Street, Savannah Rose; Designed by Tom Christ, interior designed by Marilyn Cataldie and Michael Hardy

119 Savannah Street; Designed by Robert Lamar

118 Savannah Street; Designed by Deborah Berke

117 Savannah Street; Designed by Susan Shaw

118 Savannah.

116 Savannah Street; Designed by Tom Christ

115 Savannah Street; Designed by architect Carey McWhorter

114 Savannah Street; Designed by Robert Lamar

113 Savannah Street; Designed by Ernesto Buch

112 Savannah Street; Designed by Robert Lamar

111 Savannah Street; Designed by Benoit Laurent

110 Savannah Street; Designed by Advance Planning Service

106 Savannah.

109 Savannah Street; Designed by Robert Bitterli
108 Savannah Street; Designed by Advance Planning Service
107 Savannah Street; Designed by architect Jeff Prescott
106 Savannah Street; Designed by Derrick Smith
105 Savannah Street; Designed by Highland Partners Architects
104 Savannah Street; Designed by architect Woodham Sharpe

103 Savannah Street; Designed by Tom Christ
102 Savannah Street; Designed by Derrick Smith
101 Savannah Street; Designed by Deborah Berke

At the end of Savannah Street, turn right on C-30A. Take the next right to East Ruskin Street.

103 Savannah.

East Ruskin Street (East Section)

101 E. Ruskin Street; Designed by Robert Lamar
102 E. Ruskin Street; Designed by Suellen Hudson
103 E. Ruskin Street; Designed by Derrick Smith
104 E. Ruskin Street; Designed by Straud Watson
105 E. Ruskin Street; Designed by Tom Christ
106 E. Ruskin Street; Designed by Louis Heitt
107 E. Ruskin Street; Designed by Derrick Smith
108 E. Ruskin Street; Designed by Vic Bowman
109 E. Ruskin Street; Designed by Deborah Berke

110 E. Ruskin Street, Roger's Lighthouse

Roger's Lighthouse is architect Victoria Casasco's very abstract interpretation of the Seaside Code. Ms. Casasco has explored the skeletal nature of wood frame construction, exaggerating its transparency. Visual and spatial relationships are manipulated to allow space and structure to penetrate one another. Exterior wood siding and interior plywood surfaces are superimposed over the skeletal frame like a skin. Roger's Lighthouse has been featured in several national design publications including a cover story for *Metropolitan Home.*

Front elevation of 110 E. Ruskin.

Rear elevation of 110 E. Ruskin.

Porch of 110 E. Ruskin.

111 E. Ruskin Street; Designed by Deborah Berke

112 E. Ruskin Street; Designed by Vic Bowman

113 E. Ruskin Street; Designed by Deborah Berke

114 E. Ruskin Street; Designed by Tom Christ

115 E. Ruskin Street; Designed by architect Bill Sabella

117 E. Ruskin Street; Designed by architect Rafael Pelli

116 E. Ruskin Street; Designed by architect Walter Chatham

Early in Seaside's development, the Code was not exploited to its fullest. New homeowners often mimicked existing structures, hiring many of the same architects, builders, and designers, even though the Code provided variances for "architectural merit."

One of the first who attempted to create something original while staying within the spirit of the law was New York architect and Rome Prize winner Walter Chatham. Although his cottage is unusual looking for Seaside, its massing, siting, and straightforward structural expression all conform to the town's planning mandates.

The 1,800-square-foot cottage consists of two separate, 20-foot-by-50-foot, peaked-roof pavilions that sit atop a wood plinth. The living room and kitchen are located in one pavilion; the two bedrooms and two bathrooms in the other. They are joined by a wood deck.

The two buildings are constructed of massive wood frames: paired three-inch-by-ten-inch pressure-treated pine posts and nine-inch beams, bolted together, that allow the walls to function as moveable infill panels. In good weather, the entire wall on the deck side of the buildings can be opened. The panels then function as privacy screens between the interior of the house and the street.

Living room of 116 E. Ruskin.

AT LEFT:
Front elevation of 116 E. Ruskin, designed by Walter Chatham.

83

According to Chatham, "The house functions best with all doors open, blurring the distinction between indoor and outdoor living."

The use of two separate buildings to create a single house, while unusual, is not without precedent. By separating public and private quarters, Chatham has created an abstract version of the nineteenth-century "dogtrot" house, a residential type with a breezeway that promotes ventilation during summer months. This design's advantages are increased privacy and flexibility. The separation of the bedrooms from the living and dining building also provides "a certain romantic sense of the outdoors, rather like summer camp."

The Chatham cottage was designed with passive solar cooling and requires air-conditioning only during the height of the summer. The structural system of paired three-inch-by-ten-inch wood

View from the deck into the bedrooms of 116 E. Ruskin.

columns carries a series of parallel ten-inch-by-ten-inch beams. The inner pairs of these beams support corrugated, galvanized-steel barrel vaults that form the fifteen-foot-high ceiling of each building; the outer pairs of beams support the roof. The space between the ceiling and roof is completely open. As the roof warms from the heat of the sun, the air expands and induces air from the room below to rise up to replace the warming air. The room draws replacement air from the reservoir of cool air beneath the house, cooling the room. At the same time, the space between the ceiling and roof prevents the transmission of heat into the rooms below. The rooms are also protected from direct heat gain by wide roof overhangs. Three small electric-fired heat pumps provide backup cooling and forced air heat.

Due to the nature of the site and climate (hot temperatures, salt air, and high winds), Chatham applied a number of special marine paints and finishes, including a silver marine paint for the exposed wood and walls visible at the front and back of the house, and a copper spray finish for the screen doors behind these walls. All of Chatham's decoration comes out of a paint can. "The front hall has the most beautiful ceiling in the world: the sky," he declares. Chatham avoided built-in furniture for maximum flexibility in living. His wife, furniture designer Mary Adams, designed the club chairs from blocks of foam.

The Chatham House was given an Award of Excellence by the National AIA and selected as a "Record House" by *Architectural Record* magazine.

Take the footpath between 114 and 116 E. Ruskin Street, proceed to the next footpath, and turn left. Then head south to the water.

Quincy Street/East Ruskin Street Footpath

The Seaside Motorcourt

Originally called the "No Tell Motel," the Seaside Motorcourt is an updated version of the classic motor court of early-twentieth-century America. Each unit has a queen bed, sitting area, and bath. It accommodates one or two people and is convenient to the beach.

Designed by Scott Merrill, the buildings were originally conceived as ministorage and employee parking for Town Center merchants. It grew to absorb a shipping and receiving office, a housekeeping shed, Basmati's Asian Cuisine restaurant, and the Motorcourt units themselves. A grid of sycamore trees covers the parking lot providing beautifully shaded parking spaces and a much needed lesson to designers of parking lots.

Many of the units were uniquely appointed by Kris Childs of Birmingham, who scoured the region for authentic 1940s, 1950s, and Caribbean artifacts. A number of the upholstered pieces were fabricated at Seaside by Sheri Vann and Daniel Richey.

The Seaside Motorcourt received a Florida AIA Award of Excellence in 1993.

104 E. Ruskin Street (Guest Cottage); Designed by Straud Watson

Turn right at C-30A and head west to complete this walk.

Sales and Rental Office; Designed by Scott Merrill

The Sales and Rental Office has albums with photographs of all Seaside cottages on the rental program, which you may peruse, as well as information about cottages for sale. Information about rentals may be obtained by calling (904) 231-1320 or (800) 277-8696.

AT RIGHT:
Interior of a Seaside Motorcourt, designed by Kris Childs.

Seaside Motorcourt. The logo was designed by graphic designer Peter Gordy.

WALK #3:
SEASIDE AVENUE, FOREST STREET (EASTERN SECTION), THE PARK, AND RUSKIN PLACE

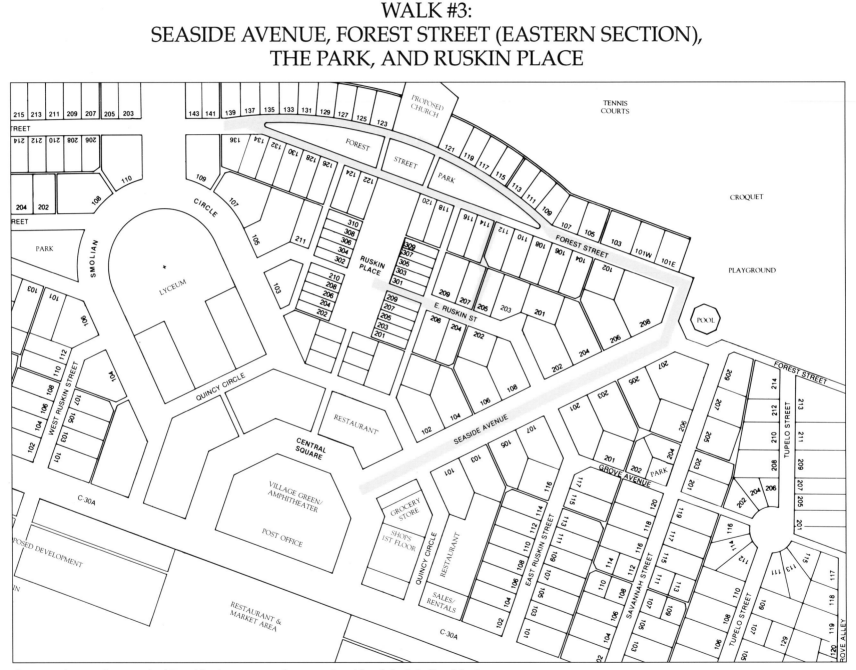

Start at the southern end of Seaside Avenue, on the opposite side of the Modica Market.

Seaside Avenue

All traditional towns have a main street or avenue that leads from the center of town to a park. The park and the avenue were used as places for promenading. In a modest-sized town, this street was usually a continuation of the main street. In a town with a town square it would more often be another street that radiated from the square. The truly grand streets had a mall, parkway, or median in the center, and the street properly became an avenue.

Robert Davis studied these street patterns in planning Seaside's grand street, Seaside Avenue. He discovered that "the best ones, those that survived the late 20th century, were not like the spectacular boulevards of the late 19th century."

The word *boulevard* derives from *bulwark* and first referred to perimeter roads just outside the city walls. These avenues were built on a giant scale for military purposes. Ironically, in the age of the automobile, Napoleon I's roads through southern Europe have fared better than Napoleon III's boulevards. With their regular plantings of cypresses from the 1820s, they look like vast cathedrals with green roofs, gigantic tree-trunk columns, and "Gothic windows" of space between the trees. Napoleon III's boulevards and those they inspired in Buenos Aires and Mexico City have not aged quite as well. Choked by traffic and lined largely with slick buildings, they are unbearably noisy and, in places, have grown a bit seedy.

Those avenues that have aged well are the smaller, more human-scaled streets with leafy trees shading the sidewalks and park benches, a sign that the internal-combustion engine and horn have not rendered them unsuitable for reading or quiet reflection.

Seaside Avenue was modelled after these successful streets. Much wider than the more modest Seaside streets, its brick sidewalks are shaded by large trees that canopy the street and reveal, at the end, the Seaside Pool Pavilion.

Seaside Avenue's houses draw inspiration from those of Greek Revival and High Victorian styles with full-width, two-story porches whose columns, along with the regularly spaced trees, establish a beautiful rhythm of vertical lines and play of light and shadow.

Seaside Avenue at night; 105 Seaside Avenue at left.

Walking on Seaside Avenue.

Seaside Avenue is designed to be experienced at a leisurely pace: strolling along the sidewalk, talking to porch sitters, bicycling to the pool, or cruising slowly in a top-down convertible.

101 Seaside Avenue

Designed by Vic Bowman, Josephine's Bed & Breakfast is a recreation of an 1840s antebellum mansion with six twenty-two-foot columns framing the front porch. It has seven bedrooms and two master suites. The rooms are furnished with period antiques, four-poster beds, balloon curtains, and Battenberg-lace-covered down comforters. Seven of the nine rooms have woodburning fireplaces.

103 Seaside Avenue; Designed by Richard Gibbs
105 Seaside Avenue; Designed by Scott Merrill
201 Seaside Avenue, Designed by Louis Heitt
203 Seaside Avenue; Designed by Don Cooper
205 Seaside Avenue; Designed by Tom Christ

Cross Seaside Avenue.

204 Seaside Avenue, Davis Residence

With the help of building inspector and draftsman John Seaborn, Robert Davis designed his own 3,500-square-foot house himself. Its clapboard siding and two stories of porches immediately recall Southern plantation houses. Like most plantation houses, it is symmetrical and axially organized. The first-floor porch opens onto the living room; the second floor opens onto the bedrooms.

Daryl Davis furnished the house with the same assured sense of style that has made her retail market, PER-SPI-CAS-ITY, an unparalleled success. She furnished the living room much like an indoor porch with wicker chairs, daybeds, and metal furniture with bright

Interior of Davis Residence, interior designed by Daryl Davis.

Exterior of 204 Seaside Avenue.

upholstery. The natural finishes throughout the house include maple floors, birch paneling, and fir trim.

Robert Davis is a wonderful cook and the kitchen is physically and symbolically at "the heart of the house." The family spends most of its time in the dining room and kitchen.

In an *Architectural Digest* interview, the Davises explained that they "wanted a house that was simple and dignified, with classical proportions and rooms, but one that also had a modern sense of spatial flow."

AT LEFT:
From right to left: 101, 103, and 105 Seaside Avenue.

Continue on to the end of Seaside Avenue, where you will come to the Pool Pavilion.

The Pool Pavilion and Recreation Facilities

The Pool Pavilion, designed by Derrick Smith, sits on an octagonal plaza from which several interconnected footpaths lead in different directions. The Pool Pavilion is the gateway to The Park, an area currently being developed as a natural preserve.

The footpaths leading from the Pool Pavilion pass through a wood, and terminate in small clearings containing a tournament-quality croquet lawn (host to National Invitational Croquet Tournaments), the Seaside Swim and Tennis Club, a small sauna and cold plunge, and, at the southern edge of The Park, an elaborate exercise pavilion with French doors opening onto a lawn for outdoor aerobics.

At the end of Seaside Avenue is the Pool Pavilion, designed by Derrick Smith.

101E Forest.

Return to the junction of Seaside Avenue and Forest Street and continue west on Forest Street.

Forest Street (Eastern Section)

101E Forest Street; Designed by Tom Christ
101W Forest Street; Designed by architects Dave Maddux/
Rick Benos
102 Forest Street; Designed by Deborah Berke
103 Forest Street; Designed by Ryce Stallings
104 Forest Street; Designed by Alan Williamson
105 Forest Street; Designed by Tom Christ
106 Forest Street; Designed by Louis Heitt
107 Forest Street; Designed by Bill Murray
108 Forest Street; Designed by Peter Horn

109 Forest Street; Designed by Louis Heitt
111 Forest Street; Designed by Louis Heitt
113 Forest Street; Designed by Tom Christ
115 Forest Street; Designed by Suellen Hudson
117 Forest Street; Designed by Richard Gibbs
127 Forest Street; Designed by Tim Terrell
131 Forest Street; Designed by Jeff Lehman
133 Forest Street; Designed by architect Eric Watson
139 Forest Street; Designed by Richard Gibbs
141 Forest Street; Designed by architect Pam Bullock

At the eastern point of the Forest Street Park, take the right fork in the road.

At the western point of the Forest Street Park, at 141 Forest Street, loop back and head east.

From left to right: 143 (designed by Charles Dunseth), 141, and 139 Forest.

AT LEFT:
117 Forest, Guest Cottage.

136 Forest Street; Designed by Pam Bullock
134 Forest Street; Designed by architect Bill Barnes
132 Forest Street; Designed by Pam Bullock
130 Forest Street; Designed by Benoit Laurent
128 Forest Street; Designed by Scott Merrill
126 Forest Street; Designed by Tom Christ
124 Forest Street; Designed by architects Shafer/Banner
122 Forest Street; Designed by Scott Merrill
120 Forest Street; Designed by Tom Christ
118 Forest Street; Designed by Tom Christ
116 Forest Street; Designed by Mark Breaux
114 Forest Street; Designed by architect Richard Dagenhart
112 Forest Street; Designed by Derrick Smith
110 Forest Street; Designed by Benoit Laurent

Take the footpath between 112 and 114 Forest Street, and continue all the way to East Ruskin Street. Turn right on East Ruskin Street, where you will find several different housing types. After exploring several of the houses on East Ruskin Street, head west toward Ruskin Place.

East Ruskin Street (Central Section)

201 E. Ruskin Street; Designed by Pam Bullock
202 E. Ruskin Street; Designed by Clay Wernicke
203 E. Ruskin Street; Designed by architects Myers/Windsor
204 E. Ruskin Street; Designed by Clay Wernicke
205 E. Ruskin Street; Designed by Derrick Smith
206 E. Ruskin Street; Designed by Tom Christ
207 E. Ruskin Street; Designed by Derrick Smith
209 E. Ruskin Street; Designed by Konrad Tamme

TOP RIGHT:
A view of Ruskin Place from E. Ruskin Street illustrates the harmonious coexistence of different housing types.

BOTTOM RIGHT:
Children playing in the Ruskin Place park.

Ruskin Place

Ruskin Place, Seaside's workshop and retail district, has expanded opportunities in the town for people to live and work. The three-story stucco buildings stand on lots twenty-one feet wide, a vivid contrast to the more traditional architecture of Seaside's cottages.

Ruskin Place is both a creative focus for Seaside's Town Center and an environment for artist colonies, creative workshops, and unusual retail shops. People on extended vacations and retired persons with arts and crafts hobbies enter comfortably into this environment. Some residents work at home.

The establishment of antique stores, designers' studios, and galleries has produced an exciting retail center. Ruskin Place is a regular host to outdoor art and music festivals.

Modelled after Jackson Square in New Orleans, Ruskin Place is Seaside's workshop district and artist colony. Its town houses share a common height but differ greatly in design and use of materials.

Architect Walter Chatham, who designed 206, 207, and 209 Ruskin Place, believes, "When it is complete, Ruskin Place will be the most urban place between New Orleans and the Atlantic Ocean. It will be as physically powerful an outdoor room as Jackson Square in New Orleans."

An art festival at Ruskin Place.

206 Ruskin Place, Martha Green Gallery.

202-204 Ruskin Place; Designed by Vic Bowman

206 Ruskin Place, Martha Green Gallery; Designed by Vic Bowman, interior designed by Martha Green

208 Ruskin Place; Designed by Walter Chatham

210 Ruskin Place; Designed by architects Luis and Jorge Trellis

302 Ruskin Place; Designed by architect Alex Gorlin

304 Ruskin Place, The Keeping Room; Designed by architect Bob Mehall

Ann Hundley and Marilou Howard offer fine-quality antique reproductions of eighteenth- and early-nineteenth-century country furniture. All pieces are handcrafted and traditional in form with contemporary colors and decorative motifs. They also carry accessories for early American and folk art collectors. Both Ann and Marilou are committed to presenting works that express the North Florida-Gulf Coast style.

Interior of The Keeping Room.

Living room/kitchen of 207 Ruskin Place.

View of the Town Center from the 207 Ruskin Place tower.

306-310 Ruskin Place; Designed by Bob Mehall

309 Ruskin Place; Designed by architect Charles Warren

307 Ruskin Place; Designed by Don Cooper

301 Ruskin Place; Designed by Alex Gorlin

209 Ruskin Place; Designed by Walter Chatham

207 Ruskin Place; Designed by Walter Chatham

205 Ruskin Place; Designed by Alex Gorlin

Other first-floor businesses include the **Newbill Collection by the Sea, Deo Favente Clothing, Mark and Penny Dragonette's Studio 210 Coffee Shop and Art Gallery,** and **Sarah Forsythe's and Dana Santi's Active Arts for Children.**

207 Ruskin Place with its glowing copper wood finish, the first Ruskin Place town house.

WALK #4: WEST SIDE

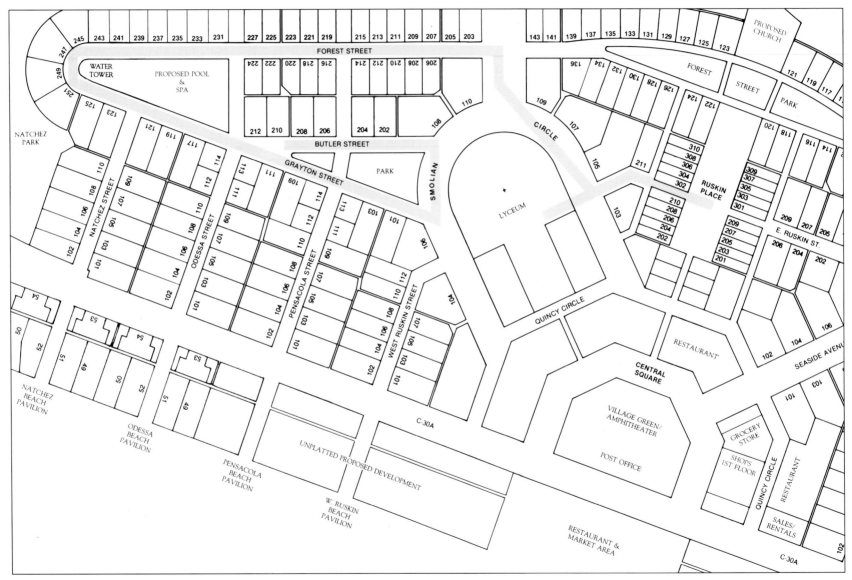

Exit Ruskin Place at the west walkway, cross Smolian Circle,
and walk into the Lyceum.

The Lyceum

Designed by architect Walter Chatham, the Seaside Lyceum campus is closely modelled on Thomas Jefferson's plan for the "academical village" of the University of Virginia (see drawing on page 51). The activities planned for the Lyceum are inspired by Jefferson's statement that "... the diffusion of light and education [is] the resource most to be relied on for ameliorating the condition, promoting the virtue, and advancing the happiness of man."

Included in Lyceum activities will be a progressive school for grades six through twelve as well as continuing education for professionals and scholars.

Exit the Lyceum from the walk-way through which you entered, and turn left onto Smolian Circle.

110 Smolian Circle.

Smolian Circle

110 Smolian Circle; Designed by Scott Merrill
The landscape plan for this cottage, designed by Clark and Charlotte Thompson, honors the natural setting.

110 Smolian Circle (Guest Cottage); Designed by Scott Merrill

Follow Smolian Circle around to the right of 110 Smolian Circle and turn left onto Forest Street heading west.

Forest Street (Western Section)

205 Forest Street; Designed by architect Robert Stanziale
206 Forest Street; Designed by Tom Christ
207 Forest Street; Designed by architect Randolph Martz
208 Forest Street; Designed by Al Lawson
210 Forest Street; Designed by Pam Bullock
212 Forest Street; Designed by Vic Bowman
214 Forest Street; Designed by architect Monica Chian

215 Forest Street; Designed by architect Sture Johanssen
216 Forest Street; Designed by architect George Israel
218 Forest Street; Designed by Pam Bullock
219 Forest Street; Designed by Jeff Prescott
224 Forest Street (Dahlgren Cottage); Designed by Charles Warren
225 Forest Street; Designed by Pam Bullock

Continue west along Forest Street to the cottages of Water Tower Place.

233 Water Tower Place; Designed by Eric Watson
237 Water Tower Place; Designed by Richard Gibbs
239 Water Tower Place; Designed by Don Cooper
241 Water Tower Place; Designed by Eric Watson
243 Water Tower Place; Designed by Eric Watson
125 Water Tower Place; Designed by Don Cooper
123 Water Tower Place; Designed by Robert Orr

At this point, the street now heads east and is called Grayton Street. Continue east along Grayton Street with the park on your left.

AT LEFT:
224 Forest.

Grayton Street and Grayton Park

121 Grayton Street; Designed by Don Cooper
119 Grayton Street; Designed by Scott Merrill
117 Grayton Street; Designed by Scott Merrill
114 Grayton Street; Designed by architect Fleming Smith III
111 Grayton Street; Designed by Gipps/Chian/Boomer
109 Grayton Street; Designed by Scott Merrill

103 Grayton Street; Designed by Scott Merrill
101 Grayton Street; Designed by Ralph Bogardus

Turn left at Smolian Circle and take the next left onto Butler Street, heading west, to complete this walk.

An overview of Grayton Street.

Butler Street

202 Butler Street; Designed by Mark Breaux

204 Butler Street; Designed by Carey McWhorter

206 Butler Street; Designed by architects Mockbee & Coker

208 Butler Street; Designed by Skip Shafer and Jeremy Kotas

210 Butler Street; Designed by architects Nonya Gernader and Rafael Pelli

212 Butler Street; Designed by Nonya Gernader and Rafael Pelli

208 Butler.

204 Butler.

212 Butler.

WALK #5: WEST SIDE RESIDENTIAL

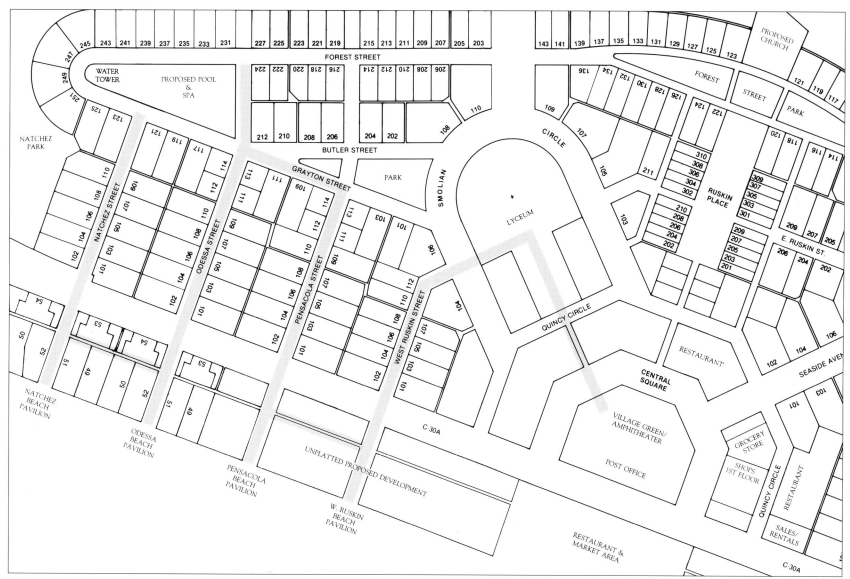

*Walk west along Grayton Street until you come to Natchez Street. Turn
left and head south toward the water.*

Natchez Street

110 Natchez Street; Designed by Earl Bush
109 Natchez Street; Designed by Tom Christ
108 Natchez Street; Designed by Gary Justiss
107 Natchez Street; Designed by Tom Christ
106 Natchez Street; Designed by Don Cooper
105 Natchez Street; Designed by architect Sam Blemling
104 Natchez Street; Designed by architect Patrick Mulberry
103 Natchez Street; Designed by Tom Christ
102 Natchez Street; Designed by architects Spitzmiller and Norris
101 Natchez Street; Designed by Don Cooper

Cross C-30A and continue toward the beach pavilion.

The Natchez Street Beach Pavilion

The Natchez Street Beach Pavilion was designed by The Jersey Devils—architects Steve Badanes and Jim Adamson. Graduates of Princeton in the early 1970s, their work reasserts an earlier arts and crafts tradition while continuing the notions of "1960s advocacy architecture."

They design and build all their projects themselves, often living on the site. Their years of work reflect their principal interest in the building process along with a genuine concern for the client, the demands of the site, ecological issues, and the application of inventive technology and available off-the-shelf materials. Accordingly, they selected locally harvested juniper for the Natchez Pavilion because of its minimal impact on the environment.

The original idea for the design was based on two classic beach icons: the umbrella and the wave. The result is a comfortable blend of natural and industrial materials. The pavilion was described by historian Ralph Bogardus as "an elegant sea monster that appears to have crawled from the sea and settled itself gracefully across the sand dunes."

Continue east along the footpath to the next beach pavilion.

The Natchez Street Beach Pavilion.

The Odessa Street Beach Pavilion

Designed by architect Roger Ferri, the Odessa Street Pavilion is a play on vernacular "stick" architecture with the diagonal wind brace used as a motif. It has been described both as an elegant beachcombers' shack, and a tropical palm-frond hut with abstracted "sheathing" resembling the Caribbean palmetto. Its fretwork porch creates kaleidoscopic visual effects that appear solid from some angles and transparent from others.

Leave the Odessa Street Beach Pavilion, cross C-30A, and head north on Odessa Street.

The Odessa Beach Pavilion was designed by architect Roger Ferri as a play on vernacular "stick" architecture.

An overview of Odessa Street.

An overview of Odessa Street with the Beach Pavilion in the background.

Odessa Street

101 Odessa Street; Designed by Gordon Burns
102 Odessa Street; Designed by Spitzmiller/Norris
104 Odessa Street, Caribbean Cottage; Designed by Don Cooper
105 Odessa Street; Designed by Patrick Mulberry
106 Odessa Street; Designed by Susan Furr
107 Odessa Street; Designed by Don Cooper
108 Odessa Street; Designed by Patrick Mulberry
109 Odessa Street; Designed by Tom Christ
110 Odessa Street; Designed by Suellen Hudson
111 Odessa Street; Designed by Vic Bowman
112 Odessa Street; Designed by Benoit Laurent
113 Odessa Street; Designed by Don Cooper
114 Odessa Street; Designed by Fleming Smith III

Turn right on Grayton Street, then right at Pensacola Street, and head south toward the water.

Pensacola Street

114 Pensacola Street; Designed by Vic Bowman
113 Pensacola Street; Designed by Tom Christ
112 Pensacola Street; Designed by Vic Bowman
111 Pensacola Street; Designed by Pam Bullock
110 Pensacola Street; Designed by Tom Christ
109 Pensacola Street; Designed by Suellen Hudson
108 Pensacola Street; Designed by Warrior Group
107 Pensacola Street; Designed by Vic Bowman
106 Pensacola Street; Designed by Tom Christ
105 Pensacola Street; Designed by Louis Heitt
104 Pensacola Street; Designed by architect Mark Mercer
103 Pensacola Street; Designed by Deborah Berke
102 Pensacola Street; Designed by Pam Bullock
101 Pensacola Street; Designed by Sture Johanssen

Cross C-30A and proceed to the beach pavilion.

The Pensacola Street Beach Pavilion

Designed by Tony Atkin, the pavilion's oversized and illuminated pelican is reminiscent of the roadside attractions of nearby Panama City.

Continue east along the footpath to the next beach pavilion.

West Ruskin Street Beach Pavilion

Inspired by the work of Robert Venturi, architect Michael McDonough designed the West Ruskin Street Beach Pavilion to be more playful than its predecessors.

Leave the West Ruskin Street Beach Pavilion, cross C-30A, and head north on West Ruskin Street.

The playful West Ruskin Street Beach Pavilion was designed by Michael McDonough.

West Ruskin Street

101 W. Ruskin Street; Designed by architect Ken Isaacs
102 W. Ruskin Street; Designed by engineer Bob Anderson
103 W. Ruskin Street; Designed by Dennis Evans
104 W. Ruskin Street; Designed by Scott Merrill
105 W. Ruskin Street; Designed by Tom Christ
106 W. Ruskin Street; Designed by Deborah Berke
107 W. Ruskin Street; Designed by Vic Bowman
108 W. Ruskin Street; Designed by Tom Christ
110 W. Ruskin Street; Designed by Vic Bowman
112 W. Ruskin Street; Designed by Don Cooper

Cross Smolian Circle, enter the Lyceum, turn right, and exit across Quincy Circle. Walk to the Village Green and Amphitheater to complete this last walk.

PREVIOUS PAGE:
The Pensacola Street Beach Pavilion was designed by Tony Atkin.

From right to left: 101, 103, and 105 W. Ruskin.

TOWN CENTER

"Plaza life is the soul of a town," wrote realtor and Panhandle resident Christopher Kent in an editorial to the *Seaside Times.* "How can we [ever] consider the modern shopping mall and food court experience . . . comparable to the atmosphere of a New England village green or a stroll along a main street in the center of a small Southern town?"

By the same token, even the small, east coast Italian town of Agropoli, with its dreary, postwar apartment buildings, expresses its vitality by virtue of its plaza life. "The town fathers of Agropoli must have figured early on that they would not draw visitors on the reputation of the town's beauty," explains Robert Davis, who visited the town, "so they made it a carnival. Every afternoon and evening, puppet shows, street theater, marching bands, street dances, bands playing on barges in the harbor, and fireworks displays fill the town's center. The evening promenade itself is a spectacle. The streets are more crowded than those in Rome. A seat in a sidewalk café is a better show than a Fellini movie."

Having seen in his travels how vibrant were the town centers of such cities as Siena, Gubbio, Orvieto, and Venice, Davis considered the Seaside Town Center one of the most critical parts of the Seaside plan. Modelled on Charleston and Savannah, the Seaside Town Center requires

Drawing by Michael Harrell of the completed Town Center.

The Town Center and Amphitheater green will eventually be ringed by other two- and three-story buildings, giving it the feel of an outdoor living room.

buildings to have three to four stories for proper definition of urban space. Smaller buildings provide small businesses with an opportunity to function in the heart of the community.

Once the Town Center is completed, all its buildings will work together to provide a communal atmosphere, giving the square the feeling of an outdoor living room. The Central Square will eventually contain most daily essentials and a great many amenities. The two major downtown Seaside buildings already completed offer, among their number of interesting shops, northwest Florida's most unusual food market, the Modica Market.

Downtown Seaside started modestly, as a collection of tables arranged flea-market style under canvas where people gathered to buy and sell fruits, vegetables, handicrafts, and flea-market items. Like the traditional daily or weekly markets of Europe that were the embryos of most Mediterranean towns, Seaside's outdoor market evolved. Its first real "store" was PER-SPI-CAS-ITY, which sold an imaginative collection of beach wear and beach gear in small stalls and whose design had been inspired by Mediterranean street markets.

The Post Office

Designed by Robert Davis, the Seaside Post Office is one of the most photographed post offices in the country and easily the most photographed building at Seaside. Although some visitors first think that it is not a real post office, it is, in fact, fully functioning and sends the Seaside postmark to all corners of the world.

The Seaside Post Office, designed by Robert Davis, the most photographed building in the town.

Eventually the Post Office will be moved to a spot northwest of the Lyceum and be replaced by a tower designed by Leon Krier.

The Amphitheater on the Green

The Seaside Amphitheater on the Green is Seaside's equivalent of a *piazza* and, like a true *piazza*, is an ideal place to relax and watch the parade of community life. It has been the site of elaborate wine and food tasting events (including one that featured Mondavi wines with a visit by Mr. Robert Mondavi), regularly scheduled concerts of classical, jazz, rock, and country music, highly competitive bike races, serious kite flying, and pickup games of soccer and baseball. At Christmas, carolers gather here.

Throughout the summer, movies are shown in the amphitheater just like in the outdoor theaters in Italian towns. The list of historic films shown at Seaside includes *La Dolce Vita, Metropolis,* and *Citizen Kane,* and films with seaside backdrops such as *Death in Venice, Suddenly Last Summer,* and *From Here to Eternity.*

The amphitheater is used as a staging area for bike races that draw both amateur and professional riders.

Dreamland Heights

Directly across from the amphitheater is Seaside's first large-scale building, Dreamland Heights, designed by New York architect Steven Holl. Significant for demonstrating appropriate zoning, it centralizes different activities within the building instead of locating them on separate pieces of land. Shops, tables for dining, and public spaces line the sidewalk; offices are located on the second floor, and residential apartments on the third. Office personnel and residents merely have to open their windows to enjoy the activity below.

Dreamland Heights, an integral part of the urban square, will have buildings constructed on both sides. Its surface decoration is abstract and economical; its plan incorporates the classical language of architecture with exquisitely wrought proportions and finely crafted details.

At the top of Dreamland Heights are eight "metaphysically inspired" hotel suites, which have been referred to as "a visionary glimpse into the Inn of the Future." For these eight residential units, Holl imagined a "Society of Strangers" and divided them into east- and west-facing groups. The five identical duplexes on the west, conceived for "boisterous" residents ("late risers who enjoy watching the action and toasting the sunset"), have generous bedrooms and ample space for parties. To the east are the residences for "melancholic types—early risers inclined to silence and solitude." These are called "The House of the Tragic Poet," "The House of the Musician," and "The House of the Mathematician." Each has a small second-floor room with a roof deck that affords exquisite views of the town and the sea from the highest vantage points in Seaside. An Entry Court is located between the two blocks of residences, as a place of encounter between the disparate occupants.

Dreamland Heights, designed by Steven Holl, was Seaside's first large-scale building. It has shops on the first floor, offices on the second, and residential apartments on the third.

109

The Entry Court between the third-floor residential apartments of Dreamland Heights.

Time magazine praised Dreamland Heights, noting that it "typifies Steven Holl's unadorned clarity and his attention to proportion." (The golden mean ratio was used to arrive at the dimensions of the windows, wall planes, and arcades.) At first, the building's austerity was controversial—a surprise to those who expected Seaside was going to include only colorful wood structures. Dreamland Heights was a dramatic demonstration that the Seaside Code allowed building types that departed from strict vernacular architecture. Robert Davis, as the developer of the building as well as Seaside, was willing to introduce contrasts and even some dissonance into the fabric of the town.

Dreamland Heights received an Award of Excellence from the National AIA, which stated, "This project understands and transforms the past while providing this young community with an inventive model for future civic buildings."

The Dreamland Heights colonnade.

SHOPPING IN DREAMLAND HEIGHTS

Named for the legendary founder of the Birmingham department-store dynasty, **L. Pizitz & Co.** is the chief purveyor of the "Seaside Style." Here is everything needed to furnish a Seaside cottage. Accessories from L. Pizitz & Co. have appeared in hundreds of the fashion and product catalogues photographed at Seaside.

Other stores in Dreamland Heights include **Fernleigh,** for antiques, **Azure,** for men's clothing, **iiis,** for imported sunglasses, and **Dawson's Yogurt.**

L. Pizitz is the chief purveyor of the "Seaside Style," with clothing and accessories for the home.

AT RIGHT:
The Seaside Meeting Hall.

The Seaside Meeting Hall

Designed by Deborah Berke, the Seaside Meeting Hall functions as a real town hall. It has hosted lectures, Seaside Symposium conferences, county zoning and planning meetings, Seaside Homeowners' meetings, storytelling programs, art exhibitions from local schools and universities, and, in 1993, the awarding of the first Seaside Prizes.

The Seaside Institute Writers' Conferences held in the Meeting Hall have featured *The Miami Herald*'s Meg Laughlin, WLRN's Meg O'Brian (*A Writer's Place/Florida Voices*), novelist Les Standiford (*Spill*), reporter Madeline Blais, Christine Bell (*The Perez Family*), poet Dara Wier, novelist James Crumley (*The Last Good Kiss*), James W. Hall (*Hard Aground*), Carolyn Forche (*The Country Between Us*), Dan Wakefield (*New York in the Fifties*), Vicki Covington (*Gathering Home*), short-story writer John Dufresne (*The Way That Water Enters Stone*), Edgar Award-winner Lynne Barrett (*The Land of Go*), and playwright David Kranes (*Criminals*).

Dawson's Yogurt.

Modica Market: Seaside's Little Italy

Alabamans Charles Sr. and Sarah Modica spent summers in the Florida Panhandle for thirty-seven years. One summer, they decided to explore County Route C-30A, where they found three modest cottages that appeared as if they had been standing there for decades. The quiet atmosphere of what was then an embryonic Seaside immediately attracted them.

The Modica family had been grocers in Alabama. After building a cottage in Seaside, they opened the beachside Sip 'n' Dip, a soda and ice-cream stand, next door to the already established Bud & Alley's Restaurant. Three years later, they opened the Modica Market, their true legacy to Seaside.

Like its counterpart in many European and American small towns, the Modica Market, designed by Deborah Berke, is a hub of community activity. Buying a paper at the Market and having coffee there with friends is part of almost everyone's daily routine at Seaside.

The Modica Market features deli sandwiches, gourmet coffees and cappuccino, outstanding wines, carefully selected produce, irresistible muffins, rare and imported cooking ingredients, their own Modica-brand spaghetti sauces, and even old-fashioned penny candy.

The Market has been featured in hundreds of articles in magazines such as *Vogue, Travel & Leisure, Travel South,* and *Conde Nast Traveler.* Charles Sr., Sarah, and Charles Jr. fill the market with warmth, charm, and grace, and have been instrumental in establishing the amiable quality of life at Seaside.

Like its counterpart in many small towns, the Modica Market is a hub of community activity.

SHOPPING IN SEASIDE

All of Seaside's businesses are owned either by residents or people who live nearby. The stores are quintessential "mom-and-pop" enterprises that reflect the character and personality of their owners. Some present Seaside businesses began there in tents or roadside stands, and eventually moved to permanent spaces. The slow, steady, incremental development of Seaside has made possible the growth of this type of shopping district. By contrast, large-scale malls are forced into relying mainly on national chains as tenants, because the leases signed by such tenants are "bankable," and the malls are built with funds from large institutional investors.

PER-SPI-CAS-ITY Market

PER-SPI-CAS-ITY is one of the most successful retail operations in North Florida and one of Seaside's biggest attractions. Its modest origins are typical of "preshopping mall" business development. The idea for such a market was directly inspired by the street markets in Verona, Mantova, and Venice.

Daryl and Robert Davis started the first outdoor market in Seaside the summer of 1981, as the Seaside Saturday Market. It had three sixteen-foot by four-foot tables covered by canvas awnings. Two or three vendors shared a table. It also included the "Chuck Wagon," a mobile truck that sold hamburgers, hot dogs, and Polish sausage.

Because of the intense summer heat, they eventually changed the market's time and format and renamed it the Seaside Saturday Sunset Scene. Robert made homemade gumbo and Daryl sold raw shrimp. The response was immediately enthusiastic because no shrimp truck would come out to their "remote" area.

AT LEFT:
Shoppers in PER-SPI-CAS-ITY.

Daryl presented the market to local merchants in Destin, Panama City, and Ft. Walton Beach using a watercolor painting and her own great enthusiasm. Twelve businesspeople agreed to become involved.

Daryl displayed vegetables in baskets lined with different-colored tissue paper. "The vegetables had to be absolutely perfect," recalls Daryl, "because they were only displayed for one day, and had to stand up to 90-degree weather and 80 percent humidity."

In the summer of 1982, the market grew to a two-day, weekend format. It was enlarged to eight tables. Jewelry and antique vendors were added. A take-out restaurant opened and summer promotions increased.

But the two-day format did not work well. When there were vendors, there would be no customers. When the customers returned, the vendors would be gone. It rained. "I spent a lot of time canning the tomatoes and strawberries that didn't sell because of the rain," recalls Daryl. "We were getting our share of Vitamin C but I was continually losing money."

In 1983 Daryl went to several military surplus stores and a few K-Marts to scout for inexpensive merchandise that would be appropriate to sell along with the vegetables. She found items such as pastel-colored web belts with brass

115

PER-SPI-CAS-ITY was modelled after European outdoor markets.

buckles and brightly colored plastic bags. "I was very limited in my inventory but the seed was planted, and I knew in what direction the market should go. I made money selling my merchandise, and I also made my first profit on my tomatoes (ninety-eight dollars). Things were looking up."

The present market was built in 1983—a series of stalls designed by architect Deborah Berke. In 1984, Daryl took on a partner, Mary Patton. The two believed in reasonable pricing and in offering merchandise not available in their geographic area. They researched the wholesale markets throughout the country to find new and unusual companies from which to buy.

"Travel clothes are a major interest of our customers," says Daryl. "They are looking for clothes that can be easily rolled up and still comfortably worn." Daryl and Mary chose easy-care apparel in natural fabrics, which they display on the market walls, hang from the ceilings, and roll up in wicker baskets. The insides of the eight-foot by eight-foot stalls are painted different pastel colors with natural canvas awnings providing shade for the outdoor market spaces. The pastel colors and ceiling fans evoke a Caribbean ambience. Each stand is set up with its own furniture and displays. Even display items are for sale. For example, customers can purchase the blouse and / or the basket in which it is rolled.

PER-SPI-CAS-ITY expanded and prospered. More stores were added. The market thrived.

SUE VANEER SHOP

Sue Vaneer's is *the* place for all Seaside memorabilia, including men's, women's, and children's wear, beach gear, posters, notecards and postcards, housewares (even Seaside refrigerator magnets), stationery, and books.

A clothing stall at PER-SPI-CAS-ITY.

Bob and Linda White's Sundog Books is one of Seaside's longest established businesses.

117

SUNDOG BOOKS

Bob and Linda White are the owners of Sundog Books, one of Seaside's oldest businesses. They offer contemporary and classic literature for all ages with an emphasis on children's books, Southern literature, books about nature and the environment, and, for those few inclement days, racks of mystery and romance novels.

4KIDZ

4KIDZ features whimsical cotton clothing for children twelve months to fourteen years. Accessories such as antique hats, fashion jewelry, and cowboy gear complement a selection of toys, music tapes, and novelty gift items.

PATCHOULI'S

Patchouli's features skin-care items, perfumes, and oils from around the world.

ARTZ

Originally, Donna Burgess set up a tent on the lawn next to Dreamland Heights to sell her watercolors. In 1993, she established a permanent base next to PER-SPI-CAS-ITY. The subjects of her work include Seaside homes, portraits, and beach scenes.

4KIDZ features clothing for children twelve months to fourteen years.

DINING OUT AND EATING IN

Bud & Alley's

Chef and artist Scott Witcoski and his partner, Dave Rauschkolb, opened Bud & Alley's in January of 1986, when they were both twenty-four years old. Together, they have developed the kind of restaurant that Robert Davis anticipated for Seaside—inviting, unpretentious, and innovative. Today, Bud & Alley's has become synonymous with North Florida and Seaside cuisine.

From the outset, Witcoski and Rauschkolb were committed to using the finest local and regional ingredients from northwest Florida. Seaside is only an hour from Apalachicola and twenty minutes from the Destin fishing docks, which supply a wide range of seafood. Freshwater lakes and rivers flow into the Gulf of Mexico only one-half mile from Bud & Alley's, providing both fresh- and saltwater fare.

Witcoski and Chef Paul Crout develop the menus, which change monthly to take full advantage of seasonal ingredients. Their influences are the rustic styles from such regions as the Mediterranean, the Basque, Tuscany, the American Deep South, and the Louisiana bayou.

Bud & Alley's is an evolving adventure for Witcoski and Rauschkolb. To research a wide variety of cuisines for the restaurant, they travel regularly to Portugal, Spain, Italy, Central America, and the Caribbean, as well as to California, New Mexico, and Miami. In addition to the main restaurant, they have opened the beachside Herb Garden Grill, featuring a special outdoor menu served under a gazebo.

Bud & Alley's has won numerous awards and is one of the most celebrated restaurants in Florida. It was featured on CNN, which praised it as "having some of the most innovative cuisine in the state." *Southern Living* called it "one of the best restaurants you will find anywhere." *Vogue*, in 1993, said it was their "favorite new restaurant in the world."

Bud & Alley's had the honor of hosting the venerable Ms. Edna Lewis's seventy-fifth birthday celebration in conjunction with the first Southern Cooking Symposium to Preserve Southern Cooking. They also assisted Ms. Lewis in the 1992 Citymeals-On-Wheels Benefit at Rockefeller Center in New York City, where the nation's finest chefs gathered to raise money for New York's homeless. Participants in Bud & Alley's new Guest Chef Program include Chef Norman Van Aiken, Chef Frank Stitt, Chef Susan Spicer, and Chef Lidia Bastianich, owner of New York's highly acclaimed restaurant Felidia.

Even though Bud & Alley's has been widely celebrated in national and European travel circuits, the unusual rapport among Bud & Alley's owners, employees, and customers still continues.

The Herb Garden Grill at Bud & Alley's, designed by architects Joan Chan and David Mohney, offers outdoor dining and a jazz quartet on weekends.

BUD & ALLEY'S BRAISED VENISON SHANKS "OSSO-BUCO STYLE"
(Recipe Courtesy of Bud & Alley's)

4 4-6 oz. venison shanks
1 cup all-purpose flour
1 cup canola oil
2 medium carrots, peeled and diced (small)
1 large yellow onion, diced (small)
3 ribs celery, diced (small)
½ bulb fennel, diced (small)
5 whole garlic cloves, crushed

4 bay leaves
8 whole black peppercorns
2 tsp. fresh crushed red pepper
1 cup Roma tomatoes, peeled, seeded, and diced
1¼ qt. brown venison or veal stock
2 tsp. chopped lemon zest
⅛ cup fresh thyme leaves

Gremolata

1 cup chopped parsley
2 tbsp. chopped garlic

2 tbsp. lemon zest

Dust venison shanks in flour. Heat canola oil in large sauté pan and brown venison on all sides, then transfer to paper towels and discard hot oil. Add to pan: carrots, onion, celery, fennel, garlic, bay leaves. Sauté until vibrant in color, then add peppercorns, red pepper, tomatoes, stock, and lemon zest. Bring to a boil, then add thyme.

Place browned shanks in a deep oven-proof dish or 8"x4" pan and pour sauce over shanks. Cover with aluminum foil and place in a 375-degree oven for 70 minutes or until fork tender. Serve with Gremolata. Serves 2.

Suggested Accompaniment

Creamy risotto, saffron rice, wild rice, or garlic mashed potatoes.
Beer suggestion: a hearty red ale.
Wine suggestion: Gogondas (Rhone Valley) 1990 or Ridge (Sonoma Valley) 1991.

BUD & ALLEY'S YELLOWTAIL SNAPPER WITH FIRE-ROASTED TOMATO-TARRAGON SAUCE
(Recipe Courtesy of Bud & Alley's)

2 2-2½-lb. whole yellowtail snapper (or available fresh white, flaky fish)

Filet and skin snapper (save bones for stock). These fish should yield 4 generous portions.

Fish Stock

4 fish carcasses
2 bay leaves
2 garlic cloves, crushed
1 medium onion, chopped
Few sprigs parsley and reserved tarragon stems (see below)

6 peppercorns
1 tbsp. salt
2 qt. water

Place the stock ingredients (except the water) in an 8-qt. saucepan. Over medium-high heat, sweat the vegetables until the onions become translucent. Add the water and bring to a boil. Simmer for 20 minutes, skimming the foam and scum. Strain through a fine sieve and cheesecloth.

Sautéing the Fish

1 cup flour
1 tbsp. sea salt
1 tsp. fresh ground pepper

4 tbsp. peanut oil
1 tbsp. butter

Dust the 4 boneless filets in the flour, sea salt, and pepper. No eggwash is needed for dusting snapper. Dust fish lightly.

Sauté the fish in peanut oil over high heat (375 degrees). Add the butter to oil shortly after placing fish in the oil. The butter helps achieve the desired crispness for sautéed fish.

Sauté first side until it is golden brown then turn it over and cook until you are just able to flake fish (no more than 2-3 minutes per side). Remove immediately and place fish on paper towels to drain. Remove excess oil from pan, reserving natural browning and fish drippings.

Pan Sauce

4 shallots, rough chopped

3 cloves garlic, rough chopped

¼ cup fresh tarragon leaves, rough chopped; stems reserved

⅓ cup dry sauvignon blanc

⅓ cup light fish stock

4 oven-roasted Roma tomatoes, rough chopped

4 tbsp. cold butter, in pieces

Salt and pepper to taste

Fresh tarragon for garnish

Immediately place pan over medium-high heat and add shallots, garlic, and tarragon leaves, tossing briefly (the tarragon aroma will be intense at this point). Add sauvingon blanc to deglaze pan, then add fish stock and roasted tomatoes. Reduce sauce by two-thirds.

Lower heat to medium and whisk in cold butter bit by bit until butter is just dissolved, taking care not to let butter break. Add salt and pepper to sauce to suit taste.

Pour sauce over fish and serve. Garnish with sprigs of fresh tarragon. Serves 4.

Wine Suggestion

Girgich Hills Sauvignon Blanc.

Basmati's Asian Cuisine

Owned and operated by Charles Bush and his wife, Shueh-Mei Pong, Basmati's Asian Cuisine is an intimate restaurant quietly secluded on Quincy Circle. Shueh-Mei, a native of Taiwan, is responsible for all the food preparation. She presents a unique combination of dishes incorporating Chinese, Japanese, Thai, and Indian cuisines.

A variety of seafood is combined with traditional herbs and spices and either pan sautéed, baked, or stir fried in light oils. Dishes are prepared in classic Oriental style, but presented with Western interpretation.

BASMATI'S CRABMEAT SALAD
(Recipe Courtesy of Basmati's)

1 lb. jumbo lump crabmeat

1 lb. cucumber, diced (home-grown summer variety is best)

¼ cup diced yellow bell pepper

¼ cup diced Vidalia onion

10-12 leaves fresh purple basil, rough chopped

12 Napa cabbage leaves

Dressing

¼ cup peanut oil

2 tbsp. rice wine vinegar

1 tbsp. soy sauce

Salt and pepper to taste

Mix crabmeat, cucumbers, bell peppers, and onion together in a medium, nonreactive mixing bowl. Add basil. Whisk together ingredients for dressing and toss with mixture. Place 2 Napa cabbage leaves on each salad plate and spoon salad equally onto leaves. Crabmeat salad and Napa cabbage leaves should be enjoyed together. Serves 6.

Shades

Located in an 1894 house moved from Chattahoochee to Seaside, Shades is the kind of neighborhood bar and restaurant you thought had disappeared forever. It offers casual, come-as-you-are family dining and entertainment, either indoors or on the porch with a commanding view of Seaside activities.

Owned and operated by Alabamans Billie McConnell and Jimmy Rogers, Shades features smoked ribs, marinated chicken sandwiches, spicy Jerk shrimp, hot dogs, and, many say, the best burger on C-30A. Shades Bar is a popular evening meeting place, especially when sporting events are televised.

SHADES SHRIMP AND TOMATO BISQUE
(Recipe Courtesy of Shades)

1 lb. butter
2 lb. medium shrimp, peeled and deveined
1 large green pepper, diced (small)
1 large red pepper, diced (small)
1 large yellow onion, diced (small)

5 medium tomatoes, diced
1 tbsp. white pepper
1 tbsp. salt
1 bay leaf
1 tbsp. seafood base
2 pt. cream

Melt butter in medium saucepan. Add shrimp, peppers, onions, and tomatoes. Cook on medium heat for 10 minutes or until shrimp are pink.

Add pepper, salt, bay leaf, and seafood base. Reduce heat. Simmer for 5 minutes.

Add cream and simmer for 5 more minutes, stirring occasionally. Remove from heat and serve as appetizer or meal. Serves 8-10.

SHADES BARBECUE SHRIMP
(Recipe Courtesy of Shades)

¼ lb. plus 1 tbsp. butter
1 tbsp. basil
1 tbsp. thyme
1 tbsp. rosemary
1 tbsp. marjoram

1 tbsp. minced garlic
5 lb. jumbo shrimp, peeled and deveined
1 5-in. section French bread

Place butter with all the seasonings in a medium sauté pan over high heat. Get this mixture very hot (about 1½ minutes), then add shrimp. Reduce heat to medium. Simmer for 3 minutes or until shrimp turn pink, stirring occasionally. *Do not overcook.*

Remove from heat. Let stand 1 minute. Serve open-faced atop French bread. Top with additional sauce. Serves 8.

The Silver Bucket

The Silver Bucket is a classic beachside sandwich-and-ice-cream shop. Originally established as the Sip 'n' Dip by the Modica family, it has been renamed and is now under the proprietorship of New Yorker Lisa Gail Smith. In addition to serving their beach customers, the Silver Bucket caters parties and other events.

LISA GAIL SMITH'S STRAWBERRY LEMONADE
(Recipe Courtesy of the Silver Bucket)

1 pt. strawberries
Lemons for ½ cup lemon juice

2 cups cold water
Ice

Sugar Syrup

½ cup water with lemon zest
½ cup sugar

Dash vanilla extract

Cook down strawberries in a saucepan. Puree in food processor. Push through sieve to remove seeds.

Squeeze lemons and pick out the seeds. Boil the sugar syrup and remove lemon zest. Mix ½ cup lemon juice with ½ cup sugar syrup.

Add 2 cups cold water. Add strawberry puree—just enough to add color. This is very sweet, so don't add too much. Stir and add ice. Makes 3 cups.

The Silver Bucket is Seaside's classic beachside sandwich-and-ice-cream shop.

RECREATION

Two of the greatest leisure indulgences at Seaside are walking on the beach and strolling through the town. Observing progress on construction is another form of Seaside recreation. Its "frontier-town vigor," as John Dixon of *Progressive Architecture* called it, provides Seaside with a constantly changing architectural landscape.

More traditional types of recreation include spring and fall surf casting with its ample rewards of whiting, pompano, and catfish. Crab netting is popular when the sea is calm. (Nets are available at the Seagrove Village Market.) Crabs can also be trapped in Western Lake. Boats for deep-sea fishing leave from neighboring Destin and Panama City. The staff at Seaside can assist in reserving a charter boat or a place on a party boat.

Seaside rents bikes by the hour, day, or week for bicycling through Seaside and along scenic C-30A. There's plenty of open sky for kite flying. High-tech and decorative Oriental kites are available at PER-SPI-CAS-ITY.

Volleyball games are on-going on the beach below Bud & Alley's. Hobie Cats and Windsurfers are also available there, as are beach chairs and umbrellas for more sedentary recreation.

The Seaside Swim and Tennis Club has six tennis courts, a croquet lawn, and three pools. Golf is available at the nearby Santa Rosa Golf and Beach Club or at Sandestin.

A run (or walk) on the beach is a favorite part of the Seaside experience.

THE SEASIDE INSTITUTE

The Seaside Institute is a nonprofit organization established in the 1980s to ensure Seaside's leadership position as a laboratory for better community planning, design, and development. The Institute also has become an important element in Seaside's development as a cultural center.

The Institute sponsors a broad spectrum of performing and visual arts, literary events, and educational programs throughout the year. It has offered chamber music, dance, poetry readings, recitals, arts and crafts exhibitions, movies, writers' and artists' workshops, photography, and storytelling. Guests have included the Ridge String Quartet, members of the New York Opera Company, and pianist Eugene Istomin.

Following are some Seaside Institute programs.

The Seaside Forum will foster development of intellectual ideas from every discipline involved with improvement of the quality of life.

The Seaside Press will publish the ideas emanating from the Seaside Forum, workshops, conferences, and other programs.

The Seaside Library will house reference materials on vernacular architecture and interior design; regional history, culture, and literature; ecology and biology of the native coastline, forest, and wetlands; and the history of the Florida Panhandle.

The Seaside Arts Program will present exhibits, lectures, readings, concerts, and training workshops conducted by a wide range of artists; it will encourage young talent and honor established masters.

The Seaside Prize is awarded annually to those people who have made significant contributions to the quality of community life. Seaside Prizes have been awarded to architect Robert A. M. Stern, architectural historian Vincent Scully, architects/town planners Elizabeth Plater-Zyberk and Andres Duany, Christopher Alexander, and the City of Portland, Oregon.

Escape to Create is a residential retreat for writers, composers, painters, sculptors, educators, and scientists. It offers a place to develop works in progress and to interact with professionals from different disciplines. One recent "Escapee" was Rome Prize-winning composer Lee Hyla.

My Town is a town meeting of Seaside Prize recipients and concerned citizens to generate ideas about how a community (the *città ideale*) can serve the mind, body, and spirit. It focuses on design, culture, commerce, health, and recreation. It explores the

Seaside Institute concerts draw people from all over the Panhandle.

establishment of guidelines for all citizens—from youths to senior citizens—to contribute to their communities in deed or resource. Seaside will become a model for responsive community activism.

Born to Be an Architect is a summer study/work program for student architects and high-school students aspiring to be architects. They will design Seaside projects, learn construction techniques, and meet with mentors to exchange ideas about the profession. Eventually, the program will extend to semester length.

This Land Is Our Land is a series of conferences, field excursions, and work programs designed to preserve virgin land and countryside, restore mismanaged rural acreage and suburban tracts, and combine natural landscape with community development.

Artscape encourages the study of visual arts and crafts and facilitates their integration into the community by designing landscape to accommodate art exhibits and providing financial support.

Architectural Interiors is a project that studies the form and function of living and work spaces, seeking environmentally responsible new designs for home, business, and marketplace.

Walk around the Block is an educational package and training workshop for elementary- and secondary-school teachers. It seeks to make appreciation of architectural design and community planning an integral part of school curricula.

Community to Community is an exchange program that brings together community leaders from around the world. It examines the Seaside experiment and aspects of life in other communities. It will afford individuals and families the opportunity to live in selected "ideal cities" (such as Pienza, Italy, and Ribe, Denmark) and to experience, firsthand, the quality of life in a desirable community.

The Point Washington Program concerns the development of 18,000 rural acres adjoining Seaside. The study provides the opportunity to construct guidelines for sensitive and positive growth management anywhere in the world through public/private partnerships.

The Fort Walton Program is the result of the Community Development Agency of Fort Walton Beach, Florida asking the Seaside Institute to help with the urban design of a six-acre bayfront parcel in downtown Fort Walton. The Institute is organizing a workshop to include faculty and students from a graduate program in urban design. The goal is to produce a schematic plan for a traditional, mixed-use neighborhood that could be developed over time by a number of small-scale entrepreneurs.

The Seaside Institute is supported by contributions. The Institute raised over fifty thousand dollars for its programs in 1993, largely through the support of homeowners. Contributions to the Institute are tax deductible and can be mailed to the Seaside Institute at P.O. Box 4730, Seaside, Fla. 32459.

NOTES ON THE PHOTOGRAPHY

During our first photographic session, Robert Davis and I stood on the porch of the Tupelo Street Beach Pavilion and discussed the best approach to photographing Seaside. We had agreed that at least one person should document the entire process from beginning to completion, and I unhesitatingly committed myself to this once-in-a-lifetime opportunity.

My work as an architectural photographer is grounded in the tradition of the Dutch and Italian *vedutisti,* or view painters. It is not a tradition of casual portrayal. I use a large-format view camera, on a tripod, which allows me carefully to control composition. I believe that there are best moments to photograph architecture, and I carefully select the seasons, times of day, and sky and shadow conditions for my views. I spent many pleasant, but frustrating, days at Seaside waiting for the rain and clouds to clear, and staring at my camera in its case.

My early photographs intentionally idealized and ennobled Seaside's simple structures. I chose direct, frontal views wherever possible to minimize distortions in the architectural proportions. Because color photography greatly emphasizes the presence of unsightly, contemporary artifacts (especially plastic ones), I deliberately avoided or removed anything extraneous that I believed to be graphically (or philosophically) intrusive. I tried to portray the buildings literally in their best possible light to convey that Seaside is exactly the kind of place where one would take the time to appreciate those fleetingly magical times of day.

As Seaside evolved, the focus of our documentation expanded from individual buildings and vignettes to streetscapes and overviews. The appropriateness of this broader approach was underscored during Robert's and my fellowship year at the American Academy in Rome. We traveled throughout Italy documenting Robert Davis's study of planned Italian towns. We observed the arrangement and scale of private and civic structures, and the dimensions of the streets. We concurred that these, rather than any one single edifice, contributed most to the formation of a humane and liveable urban fabric.

Seaside at twilight.

SUGGESTED READING

Seaside has stimulated a resurgence of interest in and commitment to the field of small-town planning. The following is a partial list of books and articles relating to this field, compiled with the assistance of Robert Davis and Kassy Keyes.

Barnett, Jonathan. *The Elusive City.* New York: HarperCollins, 1987.

Calthorpe, Peter. *The Next American Metropolis: Ecology, Community & The American Dream.* New York: Princeton Architectural Press, 1993.

Calvino, Italo. *Invisible Cities.* New York: Harcourt Brace, 1978.

Capitman, Barbara B. and Steven Brooke. *Deco Delights: The Beauty and Joy of Miami Beach Architecture.* New York: E. P. Dutton, 1988.

Easterling, Keller. *American Town Plans.* New York: Princeton Architectural Press, 1993.

Garreau, Joel. *Edge City: Life on the New Frontier.* New York: Doubleday, 1992.

His Royal Highness, the Prince of Wales. *A Vision of Britain: A Personal View of Architecture.* New York: Doubleday, 1989.

Haase, Ronald. *Classic Cracker: Florida's Wood-Frame Vernacular Architecture.* Sarasota, Fla.: Pineapple Press, 1992.

Hegemann, Werner and Elbert Peets. *An American Vitruvius: An Architect's Handbook of Civic Art.* 1922. Reprint. New York: Princeton Architectural Press, 1988.

Jacobs, Jane. *The Death and Life of Great American Cities.* 1961. Reprint. New York: Random House, 1963.

Katz, Peter. *The New Urbanism: Toward an Architecture of Community.* New York: McGraw-Hill, 1994.

Kelbaugh, Doug, ed. *The Pedestrian Pocket Book.* New York: Princeton Architectural Press, 1989.

Kostof, Spiro. *The City Assembled: The Elements of Urban Form through History.* New York: Bulfinch Press, 1992.

Kostof, Spiro. *The City Shaped: Urban Patterns and Meanings Through History.* New York: Bulfinch Press, 1991.

Krieger, Alex, et al. *Towns and Townmaking Principles: Andres Duany and Elizabeth Platerzyberck, Architects.* New York: Rizzoli, 1991.

Krier, Leon. "Houses, Palaces, Cities." In *Elements of Architecure: An Architectural Design Profile,* by Robert Krier. New York: St. Martin, 1984.

Krier, Leon. *Architecture and Urban Design 1967-1992.* London: Academy Editions, 1992.

Krier, Rob. *Architectural Compositions.* New York: Rizzoli, 1989.

Kunstler, James. *The Geography of Nowhere.* New York: Simon & Schuster, 1993.

Lewis, Roger. *Shaping the City.* Washington, D.C.: AIA Press.

Mohney, David and Keller Easterling. *Seaside: Making a Town in America.* New York: Princeton Architectural Press, 1992.

Mumford, Lewis. *The City in History: Its Origins, Its Transformations and Its Prospects.* New York: Harcourt Brace, 1968.

Prenshaw, Peggy W. and Jesse O. McKee, eds. *Sense of Place: Mississippi, A Symposium.* Jackson, Miss.: University Press of Mississippi.

Rudofsky, Bernard. *Streets for People.* New York: Anchor Press, 1969.

Rybczynski, Witold. *Looking Around: A Journey Through Architecture.* New York: Viking Penguin, 1993.

Rykwert, Joseph. *The Idea of a Town: The Anthropology of Urban Form in Rome, Italy, and the Ancient World.* 1976. Reprint. Cambridge, Mass.: MIT Press, 1988.

Sitte, Camillo. *City Planning According to Artistic Principles.* Vienna: 1889.

Stern, Robert A. M. "The Anglo-American Suburb." *Architectural Design* 51 (October/November 1981).

Unwin, Raymond. *Town Planning in Practice: An Introduction to the Art of Designing Cities and Suburbs.* 2d ed. Salem, N.H.: Ayer, 1969.

TRAVELING TO SEASIDE

Fortunately, Seaside is *not* an off-ramp exit from a superhighway. Still, it is easy to reach either by car or air.

By Air

You can fly to the general aviation airport in Destin, or you can take commercial airlines to Tallahassee, Pensacola, Panama City, or Ft. Walton Beach airports. From these you can rent a car and drive to Seaside. Tallahassee is 110 miles from Seaside; Pensacola, 70 miles; Ft. Walton Beach, 35 miles; and Panama City, 40 miles. Although the drive from Tallahassee is the longest, it does take you through some of Florida's most beautiful natural landscape. The drive from Panama City to Seaside is a sobering trip through

perhaps one of the worst-managed areas of beach development anywhere. The contrast between this strip of seacoast road and Seaside is startling.

You can be picked up and brought to Seaside from the Ft. Walton or Panama City airports by contacting Seacoast Business Services at (904) 231-4050.

By Car

Seaside is located on County Route C-30A between Grayton Beach (County Route 283) and Seagrove Beach (County Route 395). It is 360 miles from Orlando, 215 miles from Birmingham, Alabama, and 300 miles from Atlanta, Georgia.

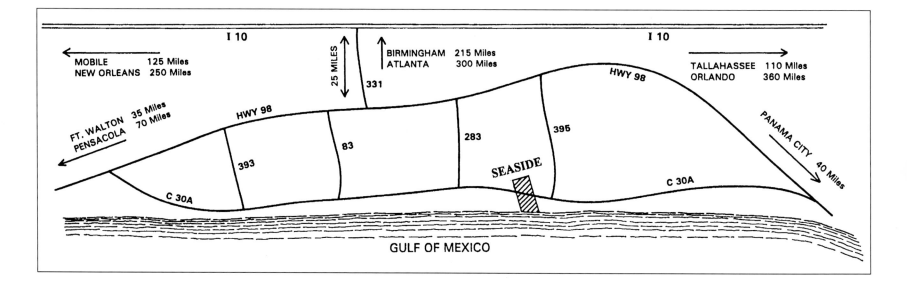